INNER VOYAGER

INNER VOYAGER

A Journal for Intuitive and Spiritual Discovery

Conceived and Edited by
Deborah Bergman

A Roundtable Press Book

SIMON AND SCHUSTER

NEW YORK   LONDON   TORONTO   SYDNEY   TOKYO

ACKNOWLEDGMENTS

Grateful and heartfelt acknowledgment is made to all those whose writings, research, and own inner voyages have added immeasurably to this book.

Simon and Schuster
Simon & Schuster Building
Rockefeller Center
1230 Avenue of the Americas
New York, New York 10020

Copyright © 1989 by Deborah Bergman and Roundtable Press, Inc.

SIMON AND SCHUSTER and colophon are registered trademarks of Simon & Schuster Inc.

Inner Voyager is A Roundtable Press Book

Directors: Marsha Melnick, Susan E. Meyer
Editorial: Patricia Fogarty
Design: David Skolkin/Binns & Lubin
Original Illustrations: Wendy Frost

Manufactured in the United States of America

10   9   8   7   6   5   4   3   2   1

Library of Congress Cataloging in Publication Data
Inner voyager.

    Bibliography: p.
    1. Spiritual life.   2. Meditations.   3. Psychical research.
I. Bergman, Deborah.
BL624.I547   1989   131   89-4313
ISBN 0-671-67846-9

This book is dedicated to all inner voyagers.

You've just finished the last class in a terrific intuitive seminar. You've made more progress than you ever imagined you could in astrology, psychic development, dreamwork, meditation, or another psychic art. The room is filled with the warmth of your fellow students, and all of you seem to be talking at the same time. In the corner, someone is asking the course leader for one final insight before the group breaks up for the last time. Looking around, you wonder how you're going to recreate all this energy and enthusiasm at home. Will your psychic skills continue to evolve as keenly without this loving support network and without regular feedback from others? Will you be able to read your hunches as well as your peers seem to? As the group files out the door, everyone exchanges addresses and phone numbers, but you can't help feeling sad and a little curious about whether you'll continue to make progress once you are on your own.

You're in the middle of a great book about past-life therapy, or one on the power of dreams. The book is affecting you in a very exciting way. You've been following some of the exercises and find they are really making a difference. For instance, sometimes you know who's on the phone before you answer it, or you take an alternate route to work on a hunch, only to find out later that there was a lengthy backup on the road you usually take. You wish you had someone you could really talk to about all of this, but your experiences are difficult to describe. You wonder how you're going to keep on developing your new skills once you finish the book.

Whether you're already deeply involved in explorations of this sort or just getting your feet wet, *Inner Voyager* will help you record and explore your intuitive development, at your personal pace and using your personal psychic talents. It provides gently structured formats, or Daily Entry pages, in which you can keep track of a year's worth of your meditation, psychic work, and daily experiences in twelve cycles, each containing twenty pages. The cycles are not dated, so you can feel free to start and stop whenever you like. At the end of each cycle, pages devoted to Inner Review help you integrate your development in all three areas, and also show you how to find and interpret your evolving personal intuitive patterns and symbols. To stimulate your work, throughout this journal you'll find inspirational quotes and descriptions of techniques from the world's intuitive traditions. And once the journal has been filled in, not only will

Nowhere can man find a quieter or more untroubled retreat than in his own soul; above all, he who possesses resources in himself, which he need only contemplate to secure immediate ease of mind—the ease that is but another word for a well-ordered spirit. Avail yourself often, then, of this retirement, and so continually renew yourself.

Marcus Aurelius,
Meditations

you have experienced a year of psychic growth, you'll also have an invaluable record of your intuitive development to treasure in years to come.

Unlocking the power of the written word

Since ancient times, the journal has been recognized as a versatile tool for spiritual exploration. Many of these personal records have produced insights so universal that they have survived to the present day, shaping the way we still perceive the Infinite or ourselves. In ancient Rome, for example, Emperor Marcus Aurelius conducted a private journey known today as his *Meditations*, a volume that describes in thoughtful detail his feelings about the role of humanity in the larger scheme of the universe. And in the fourth century, Augustine of Hippo wrote the *Confessions*, which map out some of the main thoroughfares of the inner experience with arresting poignancy and in beautiful prose.

More recently, writer Katherine Mansfield, psychologist C. G. Jung, gifted intuitive Jane Roberts, and the students of the distinguished seer Edgar Cayce have been a few of the more illustrious inner voyagers who have used journals to evolve newly discovered intuitive talents or perceptions of the uncharted dimensions of experience.

Why do so many individuals choose journals when embarking on their inner voyages? The answer is pretty straightforward: Journals are free-flowing and private. They don't require you to write or think in any particular format, or even to write at all if you have nothing to say. Although many people like to use them regularly, others keep their special books on hand just for those times when they have something particularly important to record.

When you write in a journal, you can write what you want and when you want, without anyone judging or editing the results. A journal offers a personal, protected environment, one in which you are less likely to judge yourself. This is no small consideration when you're writing about something as new and different as your psychic development! In a journal, you can feel especially free to explore all the fragments of intuitive guidance you receive, and to jot down notes about a psychic art you're beginning to develop.

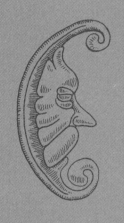

I dreamed a short story last night, even down to its name, which was Sun and Moon. *It was very light. I dreamed it all—about children. I got up at 6:30 and wrote a note or two because I knew it would fade. I'll send it some time this week. It's so nice. I didn't dream that I read it. No, I was in it, part of it, and it played 'round invisible me. . . .*

Katherine Mansfield,
Letters and Journals

No matter how frequently or infrequently you choose to use your special book, journal writing also has a natural, regular rhythm that helps order perceptions, insights, and experience into meaningful patterns. By reviewing entries regularly—but not too regularly—you will sharpen your abilities and perceptions. And by recording all your small and seemingly unrelated experiences, you will begin to amass a larger body of irrefutable evidence that your intuitive abilities and other dimensions of experience do indeed exist.

The writing process itself tends to focus psychic experiences in a deep way that yields new, more profound insight. Often, writing things down helps you to understand the experience better than you would have otherwise. Writing naturally helps focus your awareness in a way that resembles a meditative state. In that calm yet full state of mind it's easy to make new connections and uncover new insights. And since intuition expresses itself differently through each of us, the journal is not just a good format for pinpointing your talents and perceptions, but also a natural one for working out your unique relationship with tarot, I Ching, dreamwork, crystals, or any other psychic art.

Inner Voyager consists of three basic components: Daily Entries, Inner Reviews, and Inner Resources, a section at the back of the journal that provides useful information about many intuitive traditions. Each section tends to a different aspect of your growth.

Daily Entries

Each Daily Entry is divided into three sections—Meditation, Daily Experience, and Psychic Work—that can help you to clarify your experiences and impressions, and to explore the full spectrum of intuitive experience and spiritual discovery through words. Here is how it works:

Meditation

At the top of every Daily Entry page, space is reserved for you to make note of guidance and insights you receive during meditation. It's also the place to write about your progress and experiences with new meditation techniques (grounding and centering, visualization, affirmation, work with energy centers, and other practices) and to

*All hail, great master, grave sir, hail! I come
To answer thy best pleasure; be't to fly,
To swim, to dive into the fire to ride
On the curl'd clouds. To thy strong bidding, task
Ariel, and all his quality*

*Ariel,
The Tempest, Act I*

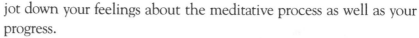

jot down your feelings about the meditative process as well as your progress.

Meditation entries can consist almost entirely of key words that describe certain experiences. For example, *Entry 1: Green light. Feeling for first time of really blending with world around me.* Entry 2: *Tingling in hands. The word "patience."* Entries can also include information that you discover while you meditate. Entry 3: *Have a feeling this is going to be a tough day at the office. Will report back later.* Entry 4: *I was right. But I also had the impression that it wouldn't affect me directly, which was also right.* You can also use the Meditation space to log impressions of different meditative techniques you try. Entry 5: *Chanting really helps me focus. Just hitting a tone or singing a song seems to work best.*

The Meditation space is also useful for recording more detailed information you receive in a guided or focused meditation, or for any other meditative purpose. If you do not meditate regularly, try using this section to write about thoughts you have and intuitive impressions you receive while you take a walk or drive to work.

TIPS FOR WRITING ABOUT MEDITATION EXPERIENCES

❧ Write quickly, without worrying about complete sentences, and use key words as shorthand for different experiences. Stay as close as you can to the meditative state as you write, and surprising new insights will flow out of your pen and into *Inner Voyager*.

❧ Describe your experiences; try not to evaluate them. If you find yourself judging, write that thought out in question form instead. Go back later and answer the questions with your first, most spontaneous impression.

❧ Once you feel comfortable with the basic process, consider making *Inner Voyager* part of your meditation. Choose a day when you will be meditating to obtain information and guidance. When you receive a first wave of information, note it in *Inner Voyager*. Focusing on the words will give you more inspiration and more questions. If you like, write the questions down. Go gently back into meditation, accept a second wave of information, and add it to the first. Continue until your communication is complete.

❧ Use *Inner Voyager* to develop such basic meditation skills as centering, becoming receptive, and stilling the mind. Describe your

experiences, and note challenge areas. Make a note to yourself that you've done this in the Inner Review section for the entry cycle. Each time you reach Inner Review, follow your reminder to go back, read each challenge, and quickly jot down a way to meet it.

OPENING A LIGHT CIRCUIT TO EASE EXPRESSION

Some people worry that they will not remember what they want to write when they are finished meditating. If you are one, try this: Before meditating, affirm, feel, see, or know that you will remember the guidance you need to write down. When you are finished meditating, imagine that a soft, gentle light in the color of your choosing is coming down through the top of your head, through your throat and heart, and moving across to your shoulder and arm and into your writing hand. This light always accesses your own inner knowledge. Then open your eyes, pick up your pen or pencil, and begin to write.

Daily Experience

Daily Experience, the second section of the Daily Entry page, is reserved for exploring the intuitive and spiritual experiences that are part of everyday events. For you, these entries might include notes on how your intuitive skills are enhancing your experiences and how they percolate through your awareness at different moments as you go about your day. Maybe you saw your child's aura, quite unexpectedly, as the two of you waited together for the school bus. Or perhaps you notice that you have developed a talent for knowing odd little pieces of information—like a name that will appear on the next page of the newspaper you are reading or what someone is about to say.

You can also use the Daily Experience space to describe how your intuition is contributing to your decisions, from the most routine to the most influential. Do you have a good feeling about one of two possible choices for a birthday present for a hard-to-fathom person, and does that feeling help you to make your choice? Does a dream give you vivid images of the outcome of a big move you might make from one part of the country to another? Once you've made the decision, you can check back to determine the accuracy of your intuitions and to refine your interpretation of them. Was the birthday present gratefully received? What was the outcome of your

A great flame follows a little spark.
Dante, Paradiso

decision to move or to stay in your present community? How did these outcomes dovetail with your intuitive insight?

These entries could also include experiences that are not directly intuitive but that appear to contribute to your spiritual growth. Everything from challenging family situations, to health problems, day-to-day career successes, and major creative triumphs may be appropriate at different moments for different people. So may gardening, traveling, playing a musical instrument, pitching a baseball, or jogging five miles along a busy city street or a snowy field.

Daily Experience entries are also useful because they are raw material to use in exploring how your meditation and psychic work experiences are percolating through your daily life beyond the protected atmosphere of your meditation corner or psychic development workshop. This wider view allows you to identify and implement more sweeping changes, progress, and attunement. Along with Meditation and Psychic Work, the Daily Experience section also provides the raw material for you to identify and enlarge the personal dictionary of intuitive symbols you may create during Inner Review (see page 16). When you work in Daily Experience, never hesitate to record fragmentary thoughts, feelings, ideas, insights, or experiences. What is elusive or merely intriguing now may become complete later in the context of *Inner Voyager* material.

Daily Experience entries can be very brief and casual. They can also be very intimate and thoughtful, like the entries from published journals you will find in the center panels of these pages. You can also combine the brief and the more contemplative approaches in a single entry, switch back and forth between the two, or invent your own special style.

TIPS FOR WRITING DAILY EXPERIENCE ENTRIES

❧ When you are not using the short-note form, experiment with writing fuller entries. Fill out a scene with details of atmosphere, the people involved, what was said, and all your insights and reflections. Don't look back as you write—keep at it until you feel a sense of completion.

❧ Review Daily Experience periodically to see if there are new intuitive talents you might want to explore more fully in the Psychic Work section.

❧ Use this section for affirmations, guided fantasies, or other work that helps you create love, self-esteem, prosperity, or other qualities you are bringing into your life. Or use it simply to write about where in your life these qualities already reside, which itself will stimulate them to manifest further.

❧ Keep track of eating habits, relationship patterns, career progress, or any other area of self-improvement that seems appropriate. Do "comfort eating" or disagreements with loved ones decrease when you're meditating regularly? Are you more productive and creative on the job when you can spend some time at your personal power spot (later in the book, *Inner Voyager* will show you how to find your power spot)? Do you feel more physically energetic or do you have greater sports endurance when you've been doing work with your higher self or with another modality of higher guidance? By comparing Daily Experience with Meditation and Psychic Work entries over several cycles, you can find out.

❧ Read the Color Attributes page in Inner Resources. Use different color pens to correspond with your subject, to harmonize with your subject, or to shift your mood.

❧ For a change of pace, try *drawing* an experience. This exercise is a refreshing break from routine that can also provide additional information, particularly if you're visually oriented.

Psychic Work

Psychic Work is the section of each Daily Entry page reserved for writing about the specific intuitive skills you may be exploring. These could be as simple as a talent for knowing who's on the other end of a ringing telephone. Or they can be as multifaceted as astrology, tarot, or work with one of the body energetics systems. Psychic Work is a good part of the entry to use when you make notes about a book you're reading or a workshop you're taking, or when you want to explore any of the psychic arts you may be getting to know, from numerology or energy channeling to shamanism or past-life work.

A list of many different kinds of psychic work appears later in *Inner Voyager* and is meant to give you an idea of the breadth of subjects that can be explored in this section of your journal.

In my sleep I saw a gothic city rising from a sea whose waves were stilled as in a stained-glass window. An arm of the sea divided the town into two; the green water stretched to my feet; on the opposite shore it washed round the base of an oriental church, and beyond it houses which existed already in the fourteenth century, so that to go across to them would have been to ascend the stream of time.

Marcel Proust,
The Guermantes Way

No matter which psychic art interests you, the first step is simply to note your experiences in the Psychic Work section when you feel the urge. You can jot them down in note form. For example, *Worked on a tarot spread with Ian—I seemed to be a little wide of the mark on career issues, although time will tell, but psychologically I "clicked" with what was going on with him—maybe this is my forte.* Or you can write more detailed descriptions of dream experiences, precognition, psychometry readings, telepathy practice with a partner, channeling, work with the earth arts through shamanism or geomancy, or whichever of the intuitive arts is speaking to you.

Don't feel that you must limit yourself to exploring just one psychic art or talent at a time. Trying things out is part of the process of getting to know what works best for you. You may also find that the different forms of psychic work address different facets of your life. For instance, you may have one or two intense experiences with past-life work (or none at all) that provide you with a dynamic dash of self-awareness at a key moment. Or, for you, past-life work may be an ongoing experience that helps you evolve your perceptions of the Infinite.

You may find yourself "cycling" quite naturally from one form of psychic work to another and then back again. If you do, just go with the flow: This very common phenomenon is an intuitive variation on the tried and true farming principle of crop rotation for greatest yield. When your skills in one area are allowed to have a fallow period, they tend to blossom forth anew with added vigor and precision. Looking back over your Psychic Work entries, you may also find that different psychic experiences are actually key pieces in a puzzle that you fit together to provide an important larger message or insight when they are seen as a whole.

If you haven't yet begun to explore a form of psychic work, *Inner Voyager* is a great place to start. The Daily Entry space gently reminds you to practice so you can develop any art into a useful and gratifying part of your life—just like playing sports or learning to cook Chinese food. And since *Inner Voyager* is your private laboratory, here you can feel free to explore a talent in solitude at the very first stages when you may feel most vulnerable, bringing it out into the world only when you're ready to do so.

Psychic Work is also the section to use for writing about skills you are developing in connection with a workshop, lecture, class, or retreat, or important insights you have about events taking place in any other protected or "classroom" environment. Perhaps for you this definition would include a healing circle, a support group, an art class, even a professional association or weekend soccer team.

TIPS FOR WRITING PSYCHIC WORK ENTRIES

❧ Try distinguishing between kinds of psychic work by using identifying initials. Label dream notes with a D, astrology notes with an A. Or record your entries for different kinds of psychic work with color-coded pens or pencils (use your own associations or refer to Color Attributes in Inner Resources). Or use personal symbols: A small rectangle could indicate a tarot entry, while a little hand could denote psychometry work. When you use initials or labels in this way, a quick glance through a month of entries will give you important additional information about your personal trends.

❧ Try using Psychic Work to deepen your understanding of the tools of your own psychic arts. Hold your favorite crystal and write about how it makes you feel or the images or events it communicates to you. The key-word method discussed in the Meditation section works fine, and so do complete sentences. Try the same technique with a crystal of a type that is totally unknown to you. Free-associate about a tarot image or a new or favorite self-healing method. If you like, warm up with the *Inner Voyager* meditation provided later in this introduction.

❧ If you're learning a healing or counseling method, use Psychic Work to make notes about sessions you give, along with the workshops and lectures you attend. Track your progress over time. Later, in conjunction with Daily Experience and Meditation, you'll be able to uncover correlations between your personal development and your sensitivity to others.

❧ It's natural to wonder whether you're just making things up when you're learning a psychic art. Here's one approach for separating insight from fantasy: As you explore your connection to each intuitive art, note the psychic impressions received and your interpretation of them. During Inner Review, go back and quickly check to see if any have panned out yet, or if any have had results other than what you had expected. Note your hits and misses on the Inner

One evening he gave us a lesson on using the I Ching. . . . He interpreted the oracular hexagrams . . . by going directly to the component trigrams and showing their relationship. . . .

He came up with mountain over thunder and . . . saw the image of a volcano about to erupt—and this was 1939. . . . Using the bowl of flowers on the table he derived a hexagram from their grouping and discussed the state of mind of the person who had arranged them.

Alan Watts,
In My Own Way

Review pages. After you've completed subsequent cycles, go back and recheck your misses, since they may have come to fruition in the interim.

INFUSING

For those times when it's not convenient to have your journal at hand, try this technique to keep subtle impressions about work in the psychic arts fresh and vivid.

When you have an experience you want to remember for later, look around the room or setting for an object or an image you find easy to associate with it. The object might be a special river stone displayed on a coffee table or an African violet blooming on a sill. The image might be the way the streetlight outside hits the icy street, or the eyes or hands of a person who is sharing this psychic work experience with you. It helps if the object or image is a simple one. Concentrate on this object or image for a moment, infusing it with all your impressions and perceptions of the experience. You can mentally list them in words or you can infuse the *whole* of your awareness—perceived as a mass of light, feeling, or sound—into the object or image. Now see the infused object being surrounded with a protective shield of light, and "set" it into your consciousness. Then let the experience go.

When you are ready to write in your journal, summon the object or image into your conscious awareness again (you may want to do this as part of a focusing meditation). As you concentrate on the object, see an opening ease into the shield of light. Experience your original fresh and vivid impressions as they flow into you again. Begin to write.

The question of context

From time to time, you may wonder which section is most appropriate for writing about an intuitive experience. For instance, if you are learning how to give reflexology sessions, notes on the session you gave your younger sister could come under the heading of Daily Experience or of Psychic Work (for most, it probably wouldn't come under Meditation). Simply place entries like these in the "current" of experience in which you would like to consider them.

Maybe it's most useful for you to see such an experience in the

context of the progress you are making in the technique. In this case, you would use Psychic Work. But perhaps it's most helpful for you to see the experience in terms of your relationship with your sister or in terms of the way you use this skill in daily life. In that case, you would choose Daily Experience. Always treat the three entry sections as a collection of new settings in which you can create a beautiful, enlightening, and unique gem that reflects your own evolving inner voyage. Consider each event a shiny little diamond, opal, tourmaline, or amethyst: Will it be shown to best advantage in silver, copper, or gold? Which will highlight its qualities so that you can best know and appreciate them? Will your therapy sessions give you more insight when recorded in the setting of your dreamwork and tarot work, or in the context of your day-to-day life? Or will the best approach be for you to change back and forth, depending on the flow of your awareness and your daily life? It's up to you.

Perfumes, colors and sounds echo one another.

Charles Baudelaire,
"Correspondences,"
Les Fleurs du Mal

Using the meditations on the entry pages

Throughout, *Inner Voyager* offers you a meditation (a quotation or an exercise) to be used in conjunction with the journal entries. These meditations will help you access special kinds of intuitive information whenever you like, without need of a special book or a workshop. You can try them as soon as you discover them, or you may file them away for another day. If you like, you can repeat them to fit your own needs. Each time you reacquaint yourself with one, it will tap a slightly different current of awareness.

Some meditations are short and simple; others are longer and more textured. With the latter, you may prefer to ask a friend to read them to you, or trade off reading all or parts of them to one another. You can also try taping the words yourself. If you develop a favorite meditation, you'll probably get to the point where you can go through the process yourself using your inner voice. At this stage, try tapping rhythmically or even humming to keep the process going at a slow, regular pace.

Inner Review

Inner Review prompts you to ask questions that help you make useful connections between Meditation, Daily Experience, and Psychic Work; identify intuitive strengths and weaknesses, current patterns, and personal symbols; and confirm your psychic experiences. It also helps you build your intuitive experiences, layer upon layer, into a blueprint for your personal psychic development that you can refer to at a glance. When you're finished with each Inner Review, you'll be refreshed and ready to cycle back into a new series of Daily Entries.

Each review is self-explanatory. You will ask yourself questions and review Daily Entries to find the answers. These answers will help you discover the personal intuitive language that will guide you through your inner voyage. This language will be made up of the following elements.

Personal symbols consist of specific feelings, images you see in your mind's eye, or words or music you hear with your inner ear that mean something in particular to you. They can have very practical, personal applications. For instance, if the word "patience" occurs to you in your meditation, it may mean you're in for a series of delays in a business deal you're eager to close. Personal symbols can also be more generalized. Seeing light twinkling in the air around you may indicate that an important opportunity is close at hand. Some symbols may be time-related for you; for instance, a gut feeling of danger may mean that a relationship is liable to go awry within the course of a couple of months, if not sooner. You will get to know your time-related symbols through experience.

Personal symbols also come in combinations: perhaps a color along with a little phrase spoken by your inner voice, or a feeling mixed with a scrap of a song. Sometimes we prefer to discover our personal symbols in the external world: Perhaps you have developed a special relationship with the arrow symbol. You know that when an arrow shape presents itself to you out of the blue (an arrow-shaped mark on a tree, for instance) you're in tune with your own guidance source. Or perhaps there is a specific rune, I Ching pictogram, or tarot card that holds a special meaning for you beyond the universal one.

Personal symbol
comes to you
person

up in the morning, such a mood is likely to match that of the people you will be in contact with that day.

Symbols like these are the bread and butter of intuitive discovery and ongoing psychic work. Professional intuitive counselors work from their own symbols and mediums as they counsel, translating them into words and real-life situations for clients. You certainly have your own personal symbols. *Inner Voyager's* Inner Reviews will help you to pinpoint them through your personal patterns.

Personal patterns are the intuitive equivalent of all those pants of the same color in your closet. They are those frequent intuitive experiences you have (those feelings, images, sounds, and lightning-fast, dead-certain intuitions) that turn out to be giving you information of a certain kind. These patterns are discovered through practice and reflection of the type that is offered in *Inner Voyager* and that you have probably been evolving on your own.

Intuitive pattern information may come to you as a matter of course. Or you may access and discover patterns as you experience the stimulation and variety of work in the intuitive arts and mediums. Your patterns may be constant from medium to medium, or they may vary. Within larger patterns, you may find smaller ones. In your life, words, music, and ambient sound may all be smaller patterns within the larger intuitive pattern of "sound." And each could give you different kinds of information. You could discover that words give you guidance on how to go about your daily activities, or that your source of guidance communicates to you through music, or that ambient sound provides information about past and future events.

Making connections between patterns and the sort of information they convey is called "patterning." You pattern when you go through a cycle of *Inner Voyager* entries to see whether intuitive impressions within a pattern tend to preview certain kinds of daily experiences. To an extent, most of us also pattern naturally as a part of daily life once we begin to develop intuitively. You probably do so now, possibly without being aware of it. As you work with your journal, you will become more aware of this natural ability and will be reminded to note down discovered patterns in *Inner Voyager*.

Each kind of specific intuitive communication within a pattern is called a symbol. For instance, if one of your patterns is visual images and a subpattern is colors, for you lime green may symbolize "growth spurt." You will get to know your personal symbols through practice as well. Patterns and symbols can change in meaning and frequency over time. They can also split like cells, becoming more precise and specific, each fresh nuance giving you new details. Inner Review introduces you to the process of discovering patterns and symbols by showing you how to find both in your entry cycles.

Confirmation is an experience that convinces you of the accuracy of your intuitive abilities or of an intuitive impression. The most straightforward type of confirmation occurs when you have a pre-monition about a daily event and then that event actually occurs. A musician gave away his old, clanky upright piano because he was suddenly certain someone would give him a baby grand by the end of the month. His friends worried. At the end of the month, a woman who was selling her house gave the musician her baby grand.

Confirmation also operates on the more interior latitudes. A woman I know attended a guidance workshop and obtained some information about her personal guides. She was skeptical about whether these guides existed independent of her own fertile imagina-tion and willingness to participate. One seemed to have told her something about her father and the words "iron horse," which she promptly put out of her mind. That weekend she dined with her father, who ordered a bottle of wine from a California vineyard previously unknown to her—a vineyard named Iron Horse.

Professional intuitive counselors often become involved in the confirmation process as well. Sometimes they give a client informa-tion that confirms the client's hunches or unearths information the pro couldn't possibly have known. Or sometimes a counselor offers advice during a session that later comes to pass in a client's life. Often an experience like the latter one becomes a person's first milestone in acknowledging a true connection to the intuitive arts.

Personal symbols like the arrow mentioned earlier often do double duty as confirming symbols. One of my friends has a special rela-tionship with the heart symbol. She knows that if she has an insight or intuitive perception and then sees something heart-shaped, the insight under consideration is confirmed. Confirmation is one aspect of what Jung called synchronicity. If you are apprenticing as a counselor or healer, you will find confirmation in feedback from those you work with.

An *intuitive strength* is a medium through which information

When I spoke of a Chinese poem in which some old of-ficial described his coming retirement to a village inhab-ited by old men devoted to the classics, the air filled suddenly with the smell of violets, and that night some communi-cator explained that in such a place a man could escape those "knots" of passion that prevent Unity of Being. . . . I can discover no apparent difference between a natural and a supernatural smell, ex-cept that the natural smell comes and goes gradually while the other is suddenly there and then as suddenly gone.

W. B. Yeats,
A Vision

comes to you more clearly, strongly, and frequently than another. Your intuitive strength could be tarot, or clairvoyance, clairaudience, or clairsentience (the images, sounds, and feelings discussed above). It could be dreamwork or shamanism or channeling. If you pay attention, you'll probably find that your intuitive strengths are multilayered. You may use runes to "see" enlightening images. You may channel your higher self, which you may hear as a voice within.

An *intuitive challenge* is a medium to which you are attracted, but one that you find challenging. You may not understand the symbols you receive through an intuitively challenging medium. One possibility is that you are not focusing high enough and are receiving intuitive "static." If you don't feel calm, peaceful, and safe while you receive the information, you should reground (that is, return briefly to your original focusing ritual and quickly reenter the meditative state), move your meditative focus higher and brighter, and try again.

Barring this, however, you need simply to discover what kind of information your "challenge medium" contains. It may be deeper, more honest information than your more facile mediums provide. It may be humanitarian information meant to serve a group. Or the impressions you receive through challenge mediums may be intended for others. Once such a medium is recognized and its symbols deciphered, it often becomes a more effortless source of intuition, and a new challenge medium crops up in its place.

Inner Resources

In the back of the book, you will find an Inner Resources section that provides useful information from different intuitive traditions, a blank record page for recording consultations, and a personal symbols glossary for you to fill in on your own. Inner Resources is available for you to consult on astrology, mythology, body energetics, crystals, color, numerology, and other important bodies of knowledge.

Customizing Inner Voyager

You will always have the *Inner Voyager* system available for your use. And it's probably a good idea to follow it for a while. But once you get to know the basic plan, you can start to vary it with your own,

Your Highnesses have an Other World here, by which our holy faith can be so greatly advanced and from which such great wealth can be drawn.

Christopher Columbus,
Letters to the Sovereigns
on the Third Voyage,
October 18, 1498

concentrating on just one or two of the three entry types on any given day, devoting more or less space to any of the three sections, and at times simply dispensing with the system in favor of what works best for you. And of course, whenever you like you can return to the root system again. Below are some ideas on how to customize *Inner Voyager* to your own needs.

If you are just beginning to discover your intuitive abilities, try following the *Inner Voyager* format closely. Be sure to complete each Inner Review. Carefully follow the exercises in bold type in the panels, concentrating on those that focus on affirmation and visualization. Treat all your perceptions with esteem.

If you are already familiar with your intuitive abilities, try departing from the format when such a change serves your needs. Use a full page for Meditation, for Daily Experience, for Psychic Work, or for another category of your own authorship. Suspend the root format, when appropriate, to take notes on a workshop or during a nature retreat. Do try to follow the basic format on other occasions, however, so you'll be able to take full advantage of Inner Review and to ensure that you note developments in all areas of your intuitive and spiritual discovery.

If you are on an advanced, apprentice, or professional level, *Inner Voyager* can provide you with a two-tiered format that places your professional development in the context of the personal, and your personal development in the context of the professional. Feel free to use Inner Review to gather insight within your own framework and to devise your own questions. Inner Review will prompt you in this process in a later cycle, or you may want to find it now and speed things up. Use Daily Experience for client notes in addition to your own experiences (or use two *Inner Voyagers*—one for professional and one for personal use) to gain awareness about the relationship between your own development and your helping skills. Earmark Psychic Work space for notes on new techniques or exchanges with peers. If you like, you can use *Inner Voyager* as an appointment book.

Provisions for an inner voyage

The rules of thumb professional writers use can be of great help to all writers. And basic intuitive techniques for connecting with a higher source of guidance can help you to focus on the steady, strong voice of the intuitive writer within. The tips and techniques that follow combine tested techniques from both worlds of experience.

When you sit down to write, always start at the top of a new white page, so that each writing experience is fresh and unique. Try not to get sidetracked by a previous entry—there will be plenty of time to review them all later. Plus you'll derive more energy, insight, and delight from reading them through all at once during Inner Review, as well as in the future.

The same goes for the writing process itself: Be good to the momentum of your perceptions and words. Suspend the critical part of your awareness as you write. Look back at what you've written only if you've been interrupted and need to pick up the rhythm, feeling, momentum, image, or concept. If you do look back, concentrate on the *essence* of the entry.

When you feel nervous or self-critical, it's good to remind yourself that many esoteric sources, including the Old and New Testaments, identify words and sound as the forces that created the universe. They're powerful elements that deserve your respect and love, like children, no matter what your inner critic may say. Remember, the analyst we all have within, used creatively, is an invaluable helper in identifying patterns and symbols and in making connections—just like the analyst or counselor without.

But also remember that any analyst anywhere needs creative impressions to go to work. Connecting with your inner analyst before you have those impressions is like turning the car key in the ignition when the gas tank is empty. Once you know how—and how long—to let your creative impressions accumulate before turning to your inner analyst, you know most of what you need to know to write well. Refining these impressions through intuitive evaluation will focus you in a new way that provides you with fresh inspiration for accumulating new creative impressions. As you've seen, *Inner Voyager* creates that momentum for you with cycles of Daily Entries separated by Inner Reviews.

Here are a few other methods for focusing on your inner writer as you sit down with your journal. Try them out when you aren't quite sure how to approach a fascinating, multifaceted experience you had, or when you feel as though you've run out of things to say or don't know how to say what you want to put down on paper.

Chögyam Trungpa,
reincarnated Lama,
"Past and Present,"
a visual poem.

INNER VOYAGER MEDITATION

Sit with your back straight and your feet resting gently but firmly on the floor. Imagine a silver-green cord of light—as thick as a tree trunk or as thin and powerful as a laser beam—burrowing down into the earth below you. See the cord send out a broad network of light roots or smaller beams that draw energy up through them, into the cord, through your spine, and up into your belly. Take as long as you like to experience the lighted cord.

When you're ready, sense the bright white light of pure energy that exists in every speck of matter around you. Focus on that pure energy source and draw it to you. Let it single out and attract the very same pure energy that exists in your every cell and that is the fabric of your higher, free-flowing awareness. Visualize that white light whirling around you and within you, above and through your head, shoulders, and neck, and down around your whole body. Feel this light merge with the green-silver light to make one seamless, soft cocoon of energy that recharges, cleanses, and protects you.

When you feel fully centered and refreshed, shift your attention to your head and neck area. Watch as the dividing line between your inner awareness and this bright, whirling creative light disappears. You are simply an extension of this bright, creative source. Now know that your thoughts and your awareness have turned into a kind of clear, living glass that merges with the creative light. This creativity will flow through the living crystal that is your body and awareness and into words on the page.

When you're ready, find the first word of your *Inner Voyager* entry and let the others flow onto the paper.

VISUALIZATION FOR GETTING UNSTUCK

When you reach a temporary logjam in your work, put down your pencil or pen, close your eyes, visualize the blank *Inner Voyager* page, and cover it with golden light. Then find the ball of light that is always over your head. Find out what color it is (ultimately, they're all white, but they change from day to day). See that ball of light come down through the top of your head, descend through your throat and chest, and run down your writing arm, leaving in its path a beautiful, clear, energized lighted path.

Know that when you touch your pen to the page you will complete the light circuit. The words that express and continue the experience you want to discuss are already there, waiting for you to uncover them. They have always been there, eager to meet you in this precise moment.

See the words there written in a blue light against the lighted page. They *are* already there. You will have your own personal and unique way of seeing those words on the page. For instance, you might see the actual letters, or the general shape and size of the words in blue. Or you might see a brilliant blue streak—like the trail of a shooting star or headlights on a highway—cover the entire page and disappear.

Feel the golden path that moves through your body and continues onto the page. Open your eyes. Start to write. With your pen or pencil, uncover the blue light words.

If you like, add the following affirmation:

As I say these words, other words that I have inside me for expressing and exploring my experience are moving from my soul, through my body, finding their rhythms, shaping my awareness, and coming to rest right here on this page.

FINDING THE WORDS IN YOUR BODY

Those who are kinesthetically oriented or who work with body energetics can loosen up by associating the experience they want to write about with a part of the body. Ask yourself where in your body you feel the experience. Where do the words exist? Near or in a particular energy center? At another part of your body that has a special significance for you? Focus on that area and feel the energy that creates those words, or the place in you where that experience is located. Visualize a tunnel of light that begins at that spot and extends to your writing hand. Into that tunnel, send warmth or coolness through which the words can travel from that place, through your hand, and out onto the page.

GETTING TO KNOW YOUR WRITING RHYTHMS

Focused writing has its own rhythm. When you're at your peak, yours will probably come in waves or short, laserlike bursts; and, when you're not, it may manifest itself in gentle, isolated details that, when quickened, bring forth little rainstorms of insight all their own.

I confess I do not believe in time. I like to fold my magic carpet, after use, in such a way as to superimpose one part of the pattern upon another. Let visitors trip. And the highest enjoyment of timelessness—in a landscape selected at random—is when I stand among rare butterflies and their food plants. This is ecstasy, and behind the ecstasy is something else, which is hard to explain. It is like a momentary vacuum into which rushes all that I love. A sense of oneness with sun and stone. A thrill of gratitude to whom it may concern. . . .

Vladimir Nabokov,
Speak, Memory

Learn to recognize these longer waves or briefer cloudbursts. A writing session may consist of one sustained wave. But more frequently it will be made up of several of these cycles, or ones with another rhythm uniquely your own. Between cycles, when you seem to run out of things to say or feel tired, get up and take a walk around the room. Stretch. Pet the cat, water a plant, check on the kids. Even turn on your favorite lively music and do a little dance with yourself! Then sit back down, take a moment to focus, and see what develops on the page. You'll probably feel sharper and refreshed. Repeat the process until you feel that your entry is truly complete.

CREATIVE WRITING YIELDS CREATIVE FOCUSING
Some inner voyagers are new to creative writing but find it a great method for intuitive growth. Others are drawn to journals because they already love to write creatively and are just beginning to explore intuition. Still others are running neck and neck in both areas. If you belong to any of these categories, remember that creative inspiration and intuitive insight are intimate partners.

One point is particularly helpful as you embark on your inner voyage. The odds are that, if you do any sort of creative writing— fiction, poetry, drama, songs, essays, or a journal, and also if you love to send and receive letters—you already know how to put yourself into that intuitive, meditative state. And you already have a personal inner voyage meditation at your disposal.

People who do creative writing tend to have creative rituals. Do you have a special place to sit when you write? Does a certain feeling come over you when you are inspired? Do personal rituals clear your mind and make it easier for inspiration to flow to you, or even create a receptive, centered state for you? Does a certain kind of music relax you and make it easier for you to delve into the subject at hand? Use the space in your first few Psychic Work entries to consider these questions. Then use the same rituals to work intuitively through writing and also to recognize your own peak moments for doing *Inner Voyager* work.

If you haven't yet explored creative writing, maybe you have creative rituals associated with another art: playing music, taking photographs, decorating a room, or planning a garden. It's definitely time to start exploring the combination of imagination and words. The goal is not to be the next Baudelaire. It's just that given your natural intuitive talent and interests, creative writing as a hobby is likely to give you a new kind of enjoyment and to enhance your intuitive insight at the same time.

Within *Inner Voyager*, you'll find many simple creative writing exercises designed to tap your intuitive depths. Try them out. If they give you pleasure and increased understanding, the next step is to try writing out some of your Daily Experience notes as if they were little scenes happening to other characters and you were the narrator. You can write these scenes in story form or in dialogue, like a dramatic scene or screenplay. Or try them as songs or poems. A good trick for getting started is to treat the process as if you were writing a letter to a wonderful friend who is very far away and to whom you want desperately to communicate some very important information.

A *few more words*

No matter what your level or background, *Inner Voyager* holds countless options for you. You are master of your awareness, and you can shape it any way you like. Think of your notes, sentences, and paragraphs as brand-new stars in a brand-new sky you are charting for the first time, and think of the patterns you discover as constellations you are drawing from heavenly body to heavenly body. Know that you can reformulate those constellations again and again without undoing those that have come before.

Anything can happen along the way. See the meditations, exercises, quotations, and Inner Resources as the compass and stars you'll use to take your bearings. Think of the Inner Reviews as islands where you can regroup and catch your breath. And consider this introduction as nothing more than a refresher course in sailing school. When all is said and done, what you have to do is simply write: It can be every day, twice a day, once a week, twice a week, or once a month, as long as it is regular. Keep at it! Play! Enjoy!

INNER VOYAGER

DAILY EXPERIENCE

PSYCHIC WORK

Move over sun and give me
                some sky
I got me some wings and I'm
                ready to fly.

American spiritual

If you do a lot of intuitive work inside, try out your favorite meditation or form of psychic work in the great outdoors on a beautiful day.

MEDITATION

DAILY EXPERIENCE

PSYCHIC WORK

Each of us has four intuitive skills. They are Intuitive Vision, Hearing, Feeling, and Double Intuition. Although we are unaware of it, we unconsciously use these skills at every moment of our lives. We use our intuition to make decisions about the world around us by tapping one or more of our intuitive senses.

The Intuitive Sense of Vision: This is the sense that allows us to see the possibilities of how situations might work out, "I can see that will work out as planned."

The Intuitive Sense of Hearing: This sense is the unexplained voice in our heads that helps us think and understand. "I was on the train and suddenly had a thought that made everything clear."

The Intuitive Sense of Feeling: This is the sense that can cause an uncomfortable feeling telling us that something is wrong when all seems to be right. "My brain says yes but my gut feeling says no go."

The Intuitive Sense of Intuition: This is the most elusive of all the senses. It is what we have come to think of as true intuition. It is simply knowing that a situation is right or wrong. It usually occurs as a sudden flash or insight. "I knew that everything would work out by September."

All of us have all four of these intuitive senses. Each of us has a unique way of using them, however. See if you can identify these intuitive personality types in yourself and in those around you.

Dr. Fran Mandell,
in Blissues,
July/August 1988

"You can shape the electromagnetic particles of reflected light to mold this Temple into a form of beauty and light that matches the images of your Higher Self. It is a sacred place. The grace of its design is created by your own pictures of the most beautiful and joyful images you can imagine. Crystalline structures, beautiful music, lush gardens—all are created by your imagination. . . .

"Begin your journey by taking several deep breaths. . . . As you breathe deeply, transport yourself in your imagination to a beautiful meadow covered with brightly colored wild flowers. . . . You can decide to climb a mountain close by and find your Temple among the trees at the very top of the mountain. . . .

"Imagine that you are now standing at the entrance to your luminous Temple of Light. . . . Create the most beautiful place you can imagine. Is there a door? Notice its color and texture. . . .

"What does it look like inside? How high are the ceilings? Does it have windows? . . . Are there rooms? How large are they? Are there crystals in your Temple? . . . Does it have a garden? . . . Do you hear any sounds of water or music or chimes around your Temple? . . .

"Choose the area in your Temple from which

you will do your work with the light. You may want a chair or a soft cushion. What direction does it face?

"What colors are in and around your Temple? Make each color more vivid and pure. Increase the light that is flowing into your Temple. . . . Do you see short bursts or pinpoints of light? . . .

"Imagine that you are surrounded with the energy of many high beings and that your soul is expanded outward and upward. Know that as you sit in your Temple your own energies are being refined. . . .

"Ask for an inner message about what is the single most important thing you could do this week to open and grow spiritually. If you have a problem in your life, ask for a new understanding of it that will allow you to move through it more easily. Ask if there is anything you can do to become even more connected with these higher energies as you move through the day.

"When you decide to leave the Temple, reach over and touch your right hand to your heart. Later, by this touch alone, you can return in an instant to your Temple. This signal gives you immediate access to it."

LaUna Huffines and Jaiwa,
Bridge of Light

MEDITATION

DAILY EXPERIENCE

PSYCHIC WORK

"You might also try imagining a great being, a master, sitting in front of you. Imagine you are looking into the eyes of the master and aligning with his or her higher vibration. See if you can hold this image and connection for at least five minutes."

Exercise from Orin and DaBen, in *Opening to Channel*, by Sanaya Roman and Duane Packer

We may develop communication with different aspects of ourselves that exist in adjacent time/space continuums through our central or core self, the soul. The soul exists beyond time and space and maintains contact between all of our aspects as the hub of a wheel contacts all of its spokes. The aspects are viewed as various lives, past to future, and from the viewpoint of the soul, alternative realities existing simultaneously. Our present life is considered to be one of these aspects, taking three dimensional form. We open the inner-mind channel to make contact with other aspects through a meditative or trancelike state.

Jane Roberts,
Adventures in
Consciousness

The Wheel of Fortune

The Wheel is a mandala, a round, unified symbol that speaks of wholeness and perfection. The Wheel brings an awareness of the rightness of things, and for a moment The Hermit sees his position on the whole journey. This cosmic perspective brings him serenity, and that reassures him. He is not alone. Forging his own part he is part of a greater plan. The perils of the coming new journey are unknown, but the journey itself has been run many times. . . . [This card's] number is X, the first of the double numbers symbolizing the perfect start of a new cycle.

Jonathan Cainer and Carl Rider on the tarot, in The Psychic Explorer

Visualize yourself as a unique rose unfolding. What color (or colors) is the rose? What shape are its petals? Explore each of them. Do any have messages written on them, pictures to look at, or do any of them give you special feelings? What is each petal beginning to tell you about your soul? What shared essences do all the petals have in common? Repeat this meditation periodically and note the results in the Meditation section of your journal.

I pondered the therapeutic purpose of exploring Catherine's past lives. Once we had stumbled into this new realm, her improvement was dramatically rapid, without any medicine. . . . The technique was similar to reviewing a childhood in conventional therapy, except that the time frame was several thousand years, rather than the usual ten or fifteen years. . . . The success of our unorthodox exploration was unquestionable. She (and others I later would treat with hypnotic regression) was being cured with tremendous rapidity.

Brian L. Weiss, M.D.,
Many Lives, Many Masters

The body of Benjamin Franklin, Printer (like the cover of an old book, its contents torn out and stripped of its lettering and gilding), lies here, food for worms; but the work shall not be lost, for it will (as he believed) appear once more in a new and more elegant edition, revised and corrected by the Author.

Benjamin Franklin,
"Epitaph on Himself"

Mainstream medicine suffers from an extreme narrow-mindedness in thinking because of its steadfast focus upon the Newtonian worldview of people as sophisticated biological machines. Vibrational healing philosophies have the unique perspective that human beings are more than flesh and blood, proteins, fats, and nucleic acids. The body would be but a pile of disordered chemicals were it not for the animating lifeforce that maintains and organizes our molecular substituents into living, breathing, thinking individuals. The lifeforce is part of the spirit that animates all living creatures. It is the so-called "ghost in the machine." It is a unique form of subtle energy that has yet to be fully grasped by the scientists of the twentieth century. This spiritual dimension is an aspect of human nature that is not taught in medical school nor well understood by most physicians. But the spiritual element is a part of human existence that must be taken into account if we are to truly understand the basic nature of health, illness, and personal growth.

Richard Gerber, M.D.,
Vibrational Medicine

There is fairly general agreement throughout the world about the appearance of the soul. Again and again it is described as a subtle vapor or a smokelike substance. The Latin word for soul, anima, comes from the Greek anemos, wind. The Latin spiritus (spirit) also stands for wind. To the Mandan Indians the soul is transparent. With the Omaha it is said to be capable of passing through solid matter. The Thompson River Salish Indians describe it as foglike. The Koyukon say it is like air or liquid. To the East Greenland Eskimos it feels soft, like a body without bones.

Holger Kalweit,
Dreamtime & Inner Space

MEDITATION

DAILY EXPERIENCE

PSYCHIC WORK

The soul has many motions,
    body one.

Theodore Roethke,
"The Motion"

Some traditions locate the soul energy over the top of the head, others at the heart or solar plexus. Mediums often describe spiritual energy entering them from the nape of the neck or through the back, near the solar plexus or kidneys. Where do you feel your soul energy most strongly? Tune into it using your favorite intuitive sense (seeing, hearing, feeling, or "just knowing") in different situations—everyday activities, meditation, psychic work—until you know for sure. Or maybe you know instantly. If so, try taking a minute to jot down some notes about that area and how you experience it.

Here is a very simple method of crystal healing you can use on yourself whenever you sense that an emotion or emotional reaction is siphoning off your energy and sense of well-being. (Anxiety, anger, hurt feelings, emotional, and even physical pain are some of the more common culprits.)

First, select a crystal for this process. The crystal will hold the feeling in question. You can find a new one, or use one already in your personal collection. It can be as big or as small as you like.

Next, pick a time of day to work with the crystal. Perhaps it will be after your regular meditation, or before or after writing in *Inner Voyager*. Hold the crystal in your right hand (pointing toward your middle finger if you have chosen a faceted stone). Now take a slow, deep breath. As you exhale, use your breath as a sensing tool. See or affirm the breath moving to the part of the body where the troublesome emotion is stored. If you wish, try a few more breaths to make sure.

Use color or sound to support your focus.

Now look at the crystal and concentrate on it. Keep sending your breath through the area in your body. See and feel that breath loosening the emotion and sending it out of you and into the crystal. Continue the process until you feel a release.

When the emotion has been completely discharged from your body and into the stone, cleanse the energy from the crystal and send it, fresh and clean, back into the universe.

Thanks to Cese MacDonald, therapist, for this technique.

MEDITATION

DAILY EXPERIENCE

PSYCHIC WORK

First, without looking back over your entries, note your impressions on what sorts of experiences are easiest and most enjoyable for you to write about.

_____

_____

_____

_____

_____

_____

_____

Next, note what kinds of experiences you felt were most challenging to express and explore.

_____

_____

_____

_____

_____

_____

Skim your entries once again. Which seem most full of detail and new discovery, the most effortless, or the most challenging? (You may be surprised by the answer.)

_____

_____

_____

_____

_____

_____

Was there an important experience you had that you did not explore at all this month? Take time out to explore it now.

_____

_____

_____

_____

_____

_____

_____

_____

_____

_____

_____

_____

_____

_____

_____

_____

_____

Date: _____

Suggestion: In the next *Inner Voyager* section, get in the habit of writing about your more challenging experiences first, when you are fresh. The more effortless ones will simply fill in around them without any extra energy on your part.

MEDITATION

DAILY EXPERIENCE

PSYCHIC WORK

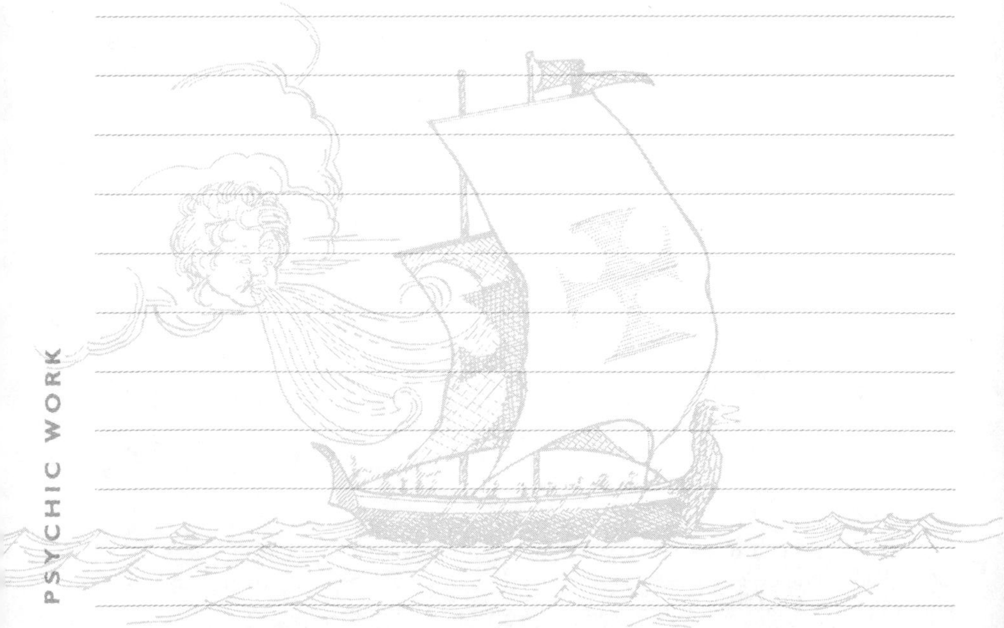

Setting out on the voyage to
Ithaca
you must pray that the way
be long,
full of adventures and experi-
ences.

Constantine Cavafy,
"Ithaca"

*It furthers a person to have
somewhere to go.*

I Ching

Psychic Synesthesia

You use synesthesia when you describe one sense impression using a second sense. If someone asks you to hum a tune that sounds pink to you, or to choose the scent that best expresses the way it feels to curl up in a big feather bed, that person would be asking you to use your sense of synesthesia. Synesthesia is used in many situations and in many forms. For instance, French Symbolist poets like Baudelaire, Rimbaud, and Mallarmé loved to use synesthesia in their poetry.

You can use psychic synesthesia to access your impressions about an important intuitive experience after the fact, as you log it in your *Inner Voyager*. It's a very useful technique if you feel a little low on energy and need an extra push to get started, or, on the other end of the energy spectrum, if it seems as though you have so many things to say you can't decide where to start.

Start by sitting in a comfortable, private place. Bring to mind the experience you'd like to write about, using visual images, words and sounds, and feelings, or by tuning into the general concept of what you want to write about.

Once it's there, pick up your pen or pencil. Then describe the experience as though it were your favorite intuitive tool. If it were a crystal, what kind would it be? An exhilarating, peak experience mountain climbing might be a large, perfect clear quartz. Success you had getting your sick child to sleep by tuning into the child's energy centers might be a pink tourmaline. What numerological value might it have (see Inner Resources for numerological values)? A whirlwind romance with a newly discovered soulmate could be a five or a two, depending on your point of view. A business success you feel you pulled off because you played your hunches instead of the hard facts could be a one, an eight, or a nine, or maybe even a four.

Describe every detail of the experience in terms of this intuitive symbol, or in terms of others that present themselves to you in the process. Gradually, other insights and perceptions about the experience in question will emerge and become a part of the synesthetic impressions on the page. Let them!

MEDITATION

DAILY EXPERIENCE

PSYCHIC WORK

*Be not afeard, the isle is full
of noises,
Sounds and sweet airs that
give delight and hurt
not.*

William Shakespeare,
The Tempest, Act III

"The best way I know to enhance High Auditory Perception is to sit for guidance. Take pencil and paper, sit in a comfortable meditative position, center yourself and lift your consciousness. Formulate a question in your mind as clearly as you can. Focus now on wanting to know the truth about that question, no matter what the answer is. Then write the question on the paper. Set the pen and paper down within reaching distance. Focus and silence the mind. Wait for an answer to come to you. After some time in silence you will begin to receive an answer. That answer will come in the form of pictures, feelings, general concepts, words or even smells. Write down the answer, no matter what it is. You may think it is irrelevant, but keep writing. The form through which the information comes will vary. Stay with it and write. The writing will eventually begin to orient the incoming information to sounds. Focus on hearing directly the words that are coming to you. Practice, practice, practice. Write everything that comes to you. Do not leave anything out. After you are finished writing, put the paper aside for at least four hours. Later, go back and read what you have written. You will find it of interest."

Barbara Ann Brennan,
Hands of Light

A relationship between a guide and a human being is a two-way phenomenon. You may be attempting to contact us, but meanwhile we've been watching you for years and years, long before you were aware of our existence. Even prior to your birth we began checking out your life plans to see if you were the one we were looking for and if it was indeed our purpose to share in your development.

If you are a member of our tribal family and we made a commitment to act as your guardian angel during this life of yours, we'll always be within hailing distance. We may make contact only once in a while, but we do approach you periodically to see how you're doing. In the meantime, we try to arrange events . . . to stimulate your own growth.

Although we may not hover continually by your side, we are with you in your hours of deepest trouble, and we stay tuned to your life situation. You are never alone. . . . The universe may scatter its children far and wide, but it doesn't abandon them. . . .

What we need from you is credibility. What you need from us is the assurance of faithfulness, of our continued good will and beneficent effect. What we need from each other is increased understanding and improved communication.

We can supply you with fresh energy and with ideas for renewing your life. We're always willing to help you develop contentment, faith, love, creativity, joyous self-expression and the flow of abundance. You in turn must be ready to permit these and all other positive qualities to manifest in yourself.

Guides Carole Judge and Marie Le Casteau, in Companions in Spirit, by Laeh Maggie Garfield and Jack Grant

The Simontons taught us how to meditate. At one point they led us in a directed meditation to find and meet an inner guide. I approached this exercise with all the skepticism one expects from a mechanistic doctor. Still, I sat down, closed my eyes, and followed directions. I didn't believe it would work, but if it did I expected to see Jesus or Moses. Who else would dare appear inside a surgeon's head?

Instead I met George, a bearded, long-haired young man wearing an immaculate flowing white gown and a skullcap. It was an incredible awakening for me, because I hadn't expected anything to happen. As the Simontons taught us to communicate with whomever we'd called up from our unconscious minds, I found that talking to George was like playing chess with myself, but without knowing what my alter ego's next move would be.

George was spontaneous, aware of my feelings, and an excellent adviser. He gave me honest answers, some of which I didn't like at first. . . .

I suppose you may call George a "meditatively re-leased insight from my un-conscious," or some such, if you must have an intellectual label for him. All I know is that he has been my invalu-able companion ever since his first appearance. My life is much easier now, because he does the hard work.

Bernie S. Siegel, M.D., Love, Medicine & Miracles

"Now ground again and ask your guide to come forward. This may take some concentrated quiet time. Though guides can arrive instantaneously, not all contacts occur right away. If you wish, phrase your request in the form of an affirmation: 'I, (name), am ready, able, and open to receive my life guide on the conscious plane.' It may not seem plausible that such simple steps can enable you to contact your guide. . . . This is not so, however. Your guide is always in readiness. . . .

"How will you experience your guide's response? Will it be through your ordinary senses? Oftentimes, yes. You may see your guide, either with your eyes closed or with them open. . . . You may hear your guide: your name spoken aloud, a line of song, a distinctive vocabulary and style of delivery. You may notice a characteristic scent, a whiff of tobacco or perfume, or perhaps a more subtle aromatic tone. You may feel a certain presence, much as you sense the vibration of someone coming up behind you. Or you may have an intuitive perception similar to that of entering a crowded room and knowing that somebody you love is in there somewhere."

Laeh Maggie Garfield and Jack Grant,
Companions in Spirit

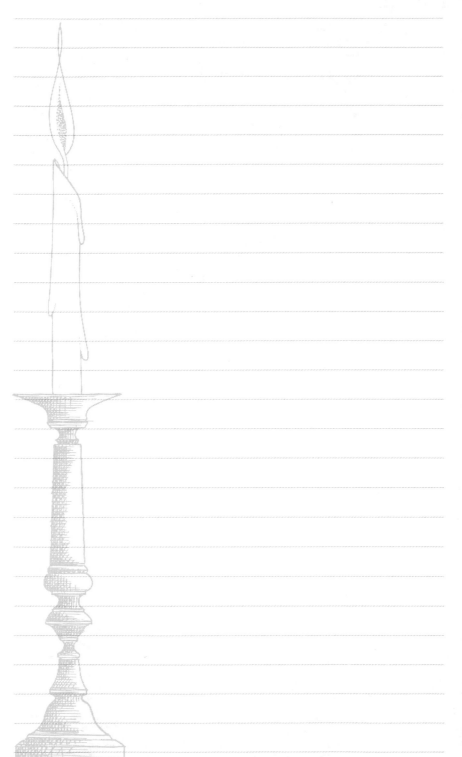

The doghouse was a small, sealed cell like a dark, frozen, airless tomb. . . . No one could withstand [it] very long, at most a few days, before beginning to ramble—to lose the sense of things, the meaning of words, and the anxiety of passing time—or simply, beginning to die. At first, huddled in her sepulcher, unable either to stand up or sit down despite her small size, Alba managed to stave off madness. . . . She gave up, decided to end this torture once and for all. She stopped eating, and only when her feebleness became too much for her did she take a sip of water. She tried not to breathe or move, and began eagerly to await her death. She stayed like this for a long time. When she had nearly achieved her goal, her Grandmother Clara, whom she had invoked so many times to help her die, appeared with the novel idea that the point was not to die, since death came anyway, but to survive, which would be a miracle. With her white linen dress, her winter gloves, her sweet toothless smile, and the mischievous gleam in her hazel eyes, she looked exactly as she had when Alba was a child. Clara also brought the saving idea of writing in her mind, without pencil or paper, to keep her thoughts occupied and to escape from the doghouse and live. She suggested she write a testimony that might one day call attention to the terrible secret she was living through. . . . "You have a lot to do, so stop feeling sorry for yourself, drink some water, and start writing," Clara told her granddaughter before disappearing the same way she had come.

Alba tried to obey her grandmother, but as soon as she began to take notes with her mind, the doghouse filled with all the characters of her story, who rushed in, shoved each other out of the way to wrap her in their anecdotes. . . . She took down their words at breakneck pace, despairing because while she was filling a page, the one before it was erased. This activity kept her fully occupied. At first, she constantly lost her train of thought and forgot new facts as fast as she remembered them. The slightest distraction or additional fear or pain caused her story to snarl like a ball of yarn. But she invented a code for recalling things in order, and then she was able to bury herself so deeply in her story that she stopped eating, scratching herself, smelling herself, and complaining, and overcame all her varied agonies.

Word went out that she was dying. The guards opened the hatch of the doghouse and lifted her effortlessly, because she was very light. They took her back to Colonel García, whose hatred had returned during these days, but she did not recognize him. She was beyond his power.

Isabel Allende,
The House of the Spirits

MEDITATION

DAILY EXPERIENCE

PSYCHIC WORK

MEDITATION

_____
_____
_____
_____
_____
_____
_____
_____

DAILY EXPERIENCE

_____
_____
_____
_____
_____
_____
_____
_____
_____
_____
_____
_____

PSYCHIC WORK

_____
_____
_____
_____
_____

At a certain point in my healing career, the guides suggested I start using black light. This seemed unusual to me, since the dark colors in the aura usually are associated with illness. This black, however, was not the black of cancer, but a velvet black, like black velvet silk. It is like the life potential held in the womb. It is the black mystery of the unknown feminine within all of us, which teems with undifferentiated life. Sitting within the black velvet void is another way to be one with the creator, but this time without form. To sit within the black velvet void means sitting in silence and peace. It means completely being there, in fullness and without judgment. It means going into a state of Grace and bringing your patient into that Grace with you. It means completely accepting everything that is in that moment. Heyoan and the other healing guides and I often sit in this place with cancer patients or other very serious illnesses for a whole hour at a time. It is very healing. It brings the patient into a state of oneness with the Divine.

Barbara Ann Brennan,
Hands of Light

Hestia was Goddess of the Hearth, or, more specifically, of the fire burning on a round hearth. . . . With Hestia, hearthkeeping is a means through which a woman puts her self and her house in order. A woman who acquires a sense of inner harmony as she accomplishes everyday tasks is in touch with this aspect of the Hestia archetypes. . . . Hestia could be glimpsed, for example, in watching a Jewish woman prepare for the Seder dinner. As she set the table, she was engrossed in sacred work, a ritual ceremony every bit as significant as the silent interchange between altar boy and priest during a Catholic mass. With Hestia as an inner presence, a woman is not "attached" to people, outcomes, possessions, prestige, or power. She feels whole as she is. . . . Hestia is an archetype of inner centeredness. She is "the still point" that gives meaning to activity, the inner reference point that allows a woman to be grounded in the midst of outer chaos, disorder, or ordinary, everyday bustle.

Jean Shinoda Bolen, M.D., Goddesses in Everywoman

If you make your own Runes, or make sets for others, let the doing be a meditation. The idea of meditating is a block for some people—including myself. I finally broke free from my anxiety about not being able to meditate conventionally when I heard mythologist Joseph Campbell say that underlining sentences in his books was his meditation. Weeding in the garden can be a meditation. So can washing your car.

Ralph Blum,
The Book of Runes

When you feel stymied or simply want to get your energy level up and loosen your journal-writing muscles, try this exercise in close description.

Choose a single object. It can be something very special—a crystal, a softly colored rock, or a perfume bottle—or it could be something very ordinary like a pencil or a telephone. It can be an object that has something to do with the experience you want to write about (the coffee table in the home where your workshop meets; the earring of the woman sitting next to you on the bus, about whom you intuited some very clear information) or it can be an object that is completely unrelated. It is, however, a good idea to keep the object as simple as possible at first. Mandalas, Bosch paintings, and car engines are probably not optimal, but it's up to you.

Hold the image of this object firmly in mind or put it in front of you. Now describe it in *Inner Voyager* as though you were describing it to someone who has just arrived on the planet and has never seen it before. Be sure to describe the shape, color, texture, feel, and all the tiny details. Really focus on describing clearly and completely. Let the object fill your entire awareness.

When you're done, begin to write your regular entry.

To see a world in a grain of
    sand
And a heaven in a wild
    flower,
Hold infinity in the palm of
    your hand
And eternity in an hour.

William Blake,
"Auguries of Innocence"

MEDITATION

DAILY EXPERIENCE

PSYCHIC WORK

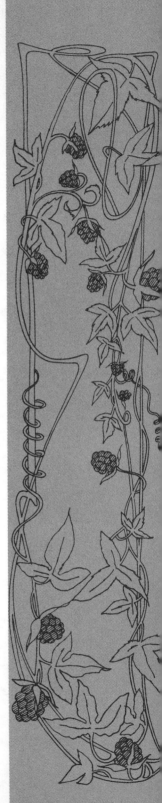

"Learn to care for a plant. Experience a deep personal relationship with it from gathering a seed to preparing the ground to talking to that seed. It holds within it a life force. The entire completed and matured plant is held within this incredible seed. . . . Clean the soil. Find out what plant will work in your environment. . . . Find a plant that you can love because of its color, its scent or because of its food, but something that you can relate to.

"Then, make a ceremony. Say a prayer, sing a song, hold the force of this life within your hands. Make a hole in the dirt and place the plant in it. Pat it over and begin to keep company with this seed and this soil. Nurture it; water it.

"As you do this, the plant becomes the metaphor for your own life. As the seed begins to grow, open, seek the light and become more that which it will be, so it is happening in your own life. Let this plant be your process as well. It will teach you everything you want to know. I don't think there is a greater teacher in all life than a single plant. We learn to slow down and observe. We learn to know wonder and gratitude. It's from a place of gratitude that all wealth is experienced."

Chequeesh Auh-ho-oh, Earth Teacher, in *Meditation* magazine, Fall 1987

Take a leisurely look through this month's entries. Is there an image, word, concept, or feeling that comes up regularly? Are there several? Write them down here. These recurring images and impressions are your personal patterns. You can use them to find out more about yourself and about how you tune in to the world around you.

Choose one personal pattern from the list. Follow it through your month of entries a second time. This time, look for connections between this pattern and the events of the month. For instance, do you experience a feeling of great warmth right before an important and very personal experience? Or did a flash of green during a meditation precede an important professional achievement or new venture you noted in Daily Experience? Write down the connection or possible connections.

Date:

Suggestion: Did your "tough" subjects get easier during this cycle? If so, pick a new one to concentrate on for the next cycle. If not, start off writing about the easy stuff for the first five entries and then switch back to focusing on your more challenging ones.

MEDITATION

_____
_____
_____
_____
_____
_____
_____
_____
_____

DAILY EXPERIENCE

_____
_____
_____
_____
_____
_____
_____
_____
_____
_____

PSYCHIC WORK

_____
_____
_____
_____
_____

Don't strain after more light than you've got yet: just wait quietly.

Evelyn Underhill, Letters

Jung . . . decided that if he really believed that the unconscious was the fountain from which all creativity sprang he would have to trust it. So he locked himself up in his room and waited on the unconscious. It wasn't long before he was down on the floor with his childish games. This led him to recall his childhood fantasies, which he then decided to express in a form of adult play. For months he labored in his backyard, building out of stone the villages and towns and forts he had fantasized as a boy. He trusted his childlike experience, and that was the beginning for him of an outpouring from the collective unconscious, from which we have the legacy of Jungian psychology.

Robert A. Johnson, He

Each of us has the ability to connect with more information than we realize. For each of us is already connected to a universal source—the Source of all awareness. Think of the source as a bustling port on an ever flowing river. The river flows through each town and village, connecting them each to the port. So, too, we each are connected to our Source—the Source of all information—through what I call The Flow. The Flow is everyone's connection to an ever-flowing, ever-informing awareness.

Patricia Einstein,
Uncommon Sense

23 February

Told him that I will try to refrain from asking too many questions, in spite of my impatient eagerness to understand, for I begin to see that he will give explanations when necessary.

"Yes; do not run after explanations, some things will be told in words, some have been told already, some are infused, no speech is necessary. They are reflected from heart to heart. Your mind knows nothing of it; but it will come up when you need it."

Irina Tweedie,
Daughter of Fire

Someday, after we have mastered the winds, the waves, the tides and gravity, we shall harness for God the energies of love. Then for the second time in the history of the world, man will have discovered fire.

Teilhard de Chardin,
Activation of Energy

*The sky glows one side black,
     three sides purple.*
*The Yellow River's ice closes,
     fish and dragons die.*
*Bark three inches thick cracks
     across the grain,*
*Carts a hundred piculs heavy
     mount the river's water.*
*Flowers of frost on the grass
     are as big as coins,*
*Brandished swords will not
     pierce the foggy sky,*
*Crashing ice flies in the swir-
     ling seas,*
*And cascades hang noiseless
     in the mountains, rain-
     bows of jade.*

Li Ho,
"The Northern Cold"

*Awake, O north wind,
     and come, O south wind!*
*Blow upon my garden,
     let its fragrance be wafted
     abroad.*

Song of Solomon 4.16

"Spirit of the North, season of winter, and place of purification, please bring your powers of renewal to our gathering. Thank you for your patience."

Jose Stevens and
Lena S. Stevens,
Secrets of Shamanism

MEDITATION

DAILY EXPERIENCE

PSYCHIC WORK

There was a time when a traveller, if he had the will and knew only a few of the secrets, could send his barge out into the Summer Sea and arrive not at Glastonbury of the monks, but at the Holy Isle of Avalon; for at that time the gates between the worlds drifted within the mists, and were open, one to another, as the traveller thought and willed. For this is the great secret, which was known to all educated men in our day: that by what men think, we create the world around us, daily new.

Marion Zimmer Bradley,
The Mists of Avalon

There is a continual shift and change within the structures of the universe that allows the planet to change. These changes are wrought, to a large degree, by the attitudes and intentions, by the consciousness, of the beings on the planet.

You must understand that thought is the creative force of your universe. . . . Its energy is available for your use. Through thought you have built the past, in thought you exist in the present, within thought you build your future.

Sheila Petersen-Lowary,
The Fifth Dimension

MEDITATION

DAILY EXPERIENCE

PSYCHIC WORK

One of the best ways to focus thought creatively is through affirmations. Affirmations are statements that shape thoughts and make a bridge between your inner and outer reality, or the world. In so doing, affirmations create a bridge that inner reality can actually cross and manifest in the outer world, into a career change, a shift in self-image, intuitive receptivity, or other phenomena.

The guidelines for making affirmations are simple. Simply frame the statement in the present tense; for example, "I have gotten the job at Adlai Stevenson and Sons I interviewed for last Thursday" or "I am channeling all the pure intuition I need to bring myself to the most appropriate level for my personal growth and balance now." Be sure to be as specific as possible. For instance, "I have my dream job now" could keep you firmly ensconced in your current position, and "I am channeling pure intuition" might simply supply you with fascinating tidbits about life in the sixth dimension that have no rhyme or reason in our world.

Inner Voyager is particularly well suited to affirmation work. Write each affirmation over and over, revising until you get it just right. Cross drafts out or label them "drafts." Repeat the honed version every day until it manifests in your life. Or try "braiding" affirmations by ending each *Inner Voyager* entry by affirming what you will write in the next entry or how you will write it. For example, "I am receiving the insight I desire about my psychic development class of last Tuesday now and I will write it in tomorrow." Or "I am receiving the answers to the questions in this entry now, and I will find out what they are as I begin to write in my *Inner Voyager* tomorrow." By braiding affirmations into a single, focused movement, you can learn to direct, shape, and manifest the ideal flow of your journal work.

"Here is an exercise you can use to muster up that 'fire in the belly' feeling on demand. (And if you think a burning creative desire is a mere figurative expression, just try it! I can tell you from experience, this exercise really fires you up!):

"Sitting with your back straight . . . imagine a great warmth at the base of your spine. Feel that warmth fill your abdominal region, moving up until it fills your entire stomach with its radiating glow.

"Now run that fire up through your spinal column in whatever color it shows itself to you (perhaps a white light, or a deep red flame). . . . Simply see and feel your spinal column as a long, firm, glowing column of heat.

"Finally, send the energy upward and outward through the top of your head, connecting it to the Infinite Creativity of Divine Creation."

Patricia Einstein,
Uncommon Sense

I dreamed such a vivid little dream of you last night. I dreamed you came to Cromford, and stayed there. You were not coming on here because you weren't well enough. You were quite clear from the consumption—quite, you told me. But there was still something that made you that you couldn't come up the hill here.

So you went out with me as I was going. It was night, and very starry. We looked at the stars, and they were different. All the constellations were different, and I, who was looking for Orion, to show you, because he is rising now, was very puzzled by these thick, close, brilliant new constellations. Then suddenly we saw one planet, so beautiful, a larger, fearful, strong star, that we were both pierced by it, possessed for a second. Then I said, "That's Jupiter"—but I felt that it wasn't Jupiter—at least not the everyday Jupiter.

Ask Jung or Freud about it? Never! It was a star that blazed for a second on one's soul.

I wish it was spring for us all.

D. H. Lawrence, in a letter to Katherine Mansfield

Try using your intuition to keep in touch with friends who aren't close physically. Try sensing for an image, voice, feeling, or other manifestation that you can interpret into information that will tell you how they are. With like-minded friends who are far away, plan a time and place to exchange intuitive information using your favorite frequency. Note the results in *Inner Voyager*, and later compare impressions by letter.

MEDITATION

DAILY EXPERIENCE

PSYCHIC WORK

Often the energy of a group of like-minded individuals magnifies and supports the energy level and focus of each individual. This is particularly true of psychic work and meditation, which is why so many people are drawn to groups and workshops when they begin to explore their psychic abilities—or study acting, or begin a professional career, or enter a new business.

As you work to divine your personal patterns and symbols in *Inner Voyager* and to describe and chart your personal intuitive growth, try getting together in small groups to interpret each other's symbols, patterns, and experiences. Record group impressions in the Psychic Work section of your journal.

MEDITATION

DAILY EXPERIENCE

PSYCHIC WORK

MEDITATION

DAILY EXPERIENCE

PSYCHIC WORK

The art of attunement to a crystal, to oneself, to another person, or to any aspect of life, is one of the most valuable tools that can be learned. Tuning in is the ability to neutralize the mind and become so still that the inner self can perceive the truth. By learning the art of attunement, we not only develop the sensitivity necessary to attain valuable inner information, but we also train the mind to communicate on much more subtle levels with different life forms. When one tunes into a crystal, the crystal becomes a mirror that will reflect the light within back into the consciousness. Meditation, visualization, physical exercise, yoga, prayer, or personal techniques can be used to calm the mind to achieve clearer perception. Whatever the approach, the results speak for themselves: greater self-control, more inner peace, personal connection to the source of truth, and the ability to have access to information that otherwise might be unavailable.

Katrina Raphaell,
Crystal Enlightenment,
Aurora Press

As you fall asleep, see yourself surrounded in a sphere of golden light, with an amethyst-colored pyramid enclosing you and the light, sealing it in. Discover how easily you slip into sleep, and experience a peaceful and regenerating night's rest.

Trace your personal patterns and symbols as you did in Inner Review 2. List them below.

_____

_____

_____

_____

_____

Now, try to make a connection between each of these symbols and an actual experience you wrote about. Note this connection below. If you don't sense strong connections, write out instead some of the key events, feelings, and insights of your cycle.

_____

_____

_____

_____

_____

_____

_____

_____

_____

_____

_____

_____

_____

_____

Did you have an experience during meditation or in a group workshop setting that was later confirmed in an everyday experience? If so, what was the form of the confirmation and how will you be able to use this experience to be aware of further confirmations in the future? If not, was this a month in which you desired confirmation? If the answer is yes, first review your entries to be certain you aren't missing anything! If not, why do you think you did not have a confirming experience?

Date:

Suggestion: In two weeks, go back and compare your symbols from question one with this monthly summary and see what connections come up at that time. Note them here. Also, refer back to this Review's symbols at the end of next month, because these events may be still to come.

MEDITATION

DAILY EXPERIENCE

PSYCHIC WORK

When many lives are re-
viewed, it is clear to see that
we have an eternity to resolve
all conflicts and karma. The
universe has infinite patience.
However, with centuries of
running into the same old
obstacles, it also becomes
clear that there is nothing like
the present to get on with
things.

Jeanne Avery, Astrology
and Your Past Lives

Your own problems are the most important ones for you to solve, for if you better your own life, you will have helped to resolve the enigma of this existence for others.

Paramahansa Yogananda

"*Spirit of the South, season of summer and place of productivity, growth, and harvest, please bring your energy and productivity to our gathering. Thank you for your warmth.*"

*Jose Stevens and
Lena S. Stevens,*
The Secrets of Shamanism

Advance to the South will be fortunate.

I Ching

Brachah leads me over to the mikvah. I take off the robe and stand expectantly in the chest-deep warm green water. Brachah tells me to keep my eyes and lips closed but not too tightly and to keep my feet and arms apart, so that the water will touch my whole body. When I go underwater I instantly curl into the fetal position because of the position of my body. When I come up, Brachah places a linen cloth over my head and I repeat the mikvah blessing after her. Then, the cloth removed, I go down two more times. The second time down, I see a little speeded-up movie of all the religious people I know, performing this ritual. I think of all the generations of people I have not known who have considered the impurities of the world dissolvable. My grandmother floats by, curled up, like me, like a little pink shrimp. I see her as she was in her very old age, senile and mute, curled up in the same position on her bed. The third time down, I think of my boys suspended inside me, waiting to join the world. I look up and see Brachah's smiling face through the water. I feel good.

Lis Harris, Holy Days

MEDITATION

DAILY EXPERIENCE

PSYCHIC WORK

In the world there is nothing more submissive and weak than water. Yet for attacking that which is hard and strong nothing can surpass it. This is because there is nothing that can take its place.

Lao Tzu, Tao Te Ching

After sudden rain, a clear
autumn night.
On golden waves the sparkle
of the Jewelled Cord.
The River of Heaven white
from eternity,
The Yangtse's shallows limpid
since just now.
Reflections, pearls from a
snapped string:
High in the sky one mirror
rises.
Afterlight which fades as the
clock drips,
Still fainter as the dewdrops
settle on the flowers.

Tu Fu,
"Stars and Moon
on the Yangtse"

In the card of the Moon, we
find in the image of Hecate
[the moon goddess] an experience of the great collective sea
of the unconscious from
which not only the individual
but the whole of life has
emerged. . . . She embodies
the feminine principle in life
itself. . . . It is from this
oceanic realm of the human
imagination that the great
myths and religious symbols
and works of art are born
over the centuries. . . .
The meeting with Hecate, the
moon-goddess, is a con-
frontation with a transper-
sonal world, where individual
boundaries dissolve and the
sense of direction and ego are
lost. . . . Something has
washed over us which
cleanses the past and prepares
the way for the future, but we
must wait as the foetus waits
in the womb. The only road
to Hecate's world is the "royal
road" of dreams.

Juliet Sharman Burke
and Liz Greene,
The Mythic Tarot

The dream is the small hidden door in the deepest and most intimate sanctum of the soul, which opens into that primeval cosmic night that was soul long before there was a conscious ego and will be soul far beyond what a conscious ego could ever reach.

C. G. Jung,
The Meaning of Psychology
for Modern Man

If you use *Inner Voyager* for dreamwork, make sure to keep it at the side of your bed so you can reach for it early in the morning to record your dreams while they are fresh. No matter what sort of information and insight comes through to you personally in your dreams (for some it's precognitive, others get ideas for their work or relationships, others find it's deeply healing on a spiritual level), you can make affirmations to shape the subject of your dreamwork.

For instance, just as language students often dream they are speaking effortlessly in their new language before they do so while awake, you may find you are channeling, receiving healing, visualizing, or performing any chosen psychic art effortlessly in dreams before you have experienced these manifestations in a waking state. Again, consider this a sign of very strong and deep progress, and perhaps also consider it a message from your chosen form of higher guidance that the psychic art in question is one you should pursue. You may want to affirm this experience using the most appropriate psychic art for you when the right moment arrives.

Animal Dream Song

See us, see us,
In your adjacent world.
We are your dreams living
In fur and blood.
We are the animals
Blessed and holy,
Savage and bony,
Thrust out by you
Into the world.

We sing your praises.
It is good common sense,
For we know that we come
From the ribs of your
        slumber,
Born, torn, and rent
From desires
Glowing and raging.

In the midnight of your senses
We rise up all splendid.
Perfect and agile
We leap out into the forests
We race across the landscapes
In moonlight and shadow.
We are your dreams escaping
The dream cage forever.
The door is wide open. . . .

Our dreams rise up
Even as yours, and confront
    us.
The animals' animals
Must be nourished and
    tended.
The dreams' dreams are not
    orphans
To be cast into darkness.

We congregate before you
For your attention.
We are the blood and hide
Of your dreams prancing
In midday.
We plunge through forests
And hillsides,
Carved out of your unknow-
    ing.
Beneath the moon of your
    brain.

Jane Roberts,
The Education of
Oversoul Seven

MEDITATION

DAILY EXPERIENCE

PSYCHIC WORK

**Waxing Moon
Meditation**

"Ground and center. Vi-
sualize a silver crescent
moon, curving to the
right. She is the power of
beginning, of growth and
generation. She is wild
and untamed, like ideas
and plans before they are
tempered by reality. She
is the blank page, the
unplowed field. Feel your
own hidden possibilities
and latent potentials;
your power to begin and
grow. See her as a silver-
haired girl running freely
through the forest under
the slim moon. She is
Virgin, eternally unpene-
trated, belonging to no
one but herself. Call her
name 'Nimue!' and feel
her power within you."

**Starhawk,
*The Spiral Dance***

The hero, the saving quality,
comes from the place where
you least expect it. . . . this
boy's name is Parsifal, which
means "innocent fool."

   It is a humbling thing for a
Fisher King to rely on his
Parsifal nature for his salvation. It's a bit like the Biblical
injunction, "Except ye become as a little child, ye
cannot enter the Kingdom of
Heaven." Unless you will
trust your Parsifal nature for
your redemption, there is no
hope for you. This comes
hard for a man, for his
masculine pride bites the
dust.

Robert A. Johnson, He

MEDITATION

DAILY EXPERIENCE

PSYCHIC WORK

One morning in Montreal I made seventeen phone calls, confirming, altering, adding and eliminating. When I came into the room where everybody was gathered I was probably palpably crackling with electricity and irritation. He [Taisen Deshimaru, the Soto Zen Master] shot a sizing-up glance from under heavy lids and, leaving the conversation to eddy on around, grabbed one of my feet and then the other and roughly, brusquely massaged away the telephone calls, one by one, leaving me gasping and grateful on the floor.

What matters is that the whole atmosphere should be in harmony; so what is showing compassion for one jarring energy is also acting in the general interest, or self-interest. They are not separate in the Oriental social code or mentality. We, with our categorizing morality, want to distinguish between compassion and self-interest; but, in fact, no such distinction exists.

Nan Shin,
Diary of a Zen Nun

MEDITATION

DAILY EXPERIENCE

PSYCHIC WORK

Use *Inner Voyager* to keep in touch with those who seem far away. The distance may be geographical, the space between one who is in body and one who is in spirit, or an emotional distance you would like to cross. Sit down to write a letter to the person in question. (Use the Daily Experience or Psychic Work section, depending on the context you prefer.) Now tell the person exactly what you have been wanting to tell them. Focus on keeping your words direct. Really concentrate on emptying your heart of the feeling in question. When you are finished, close *Inner Voyager* and do a focusing meditation. When you're ready, see, hear, feel, or intuitively just know that you are sending your message to its intended recipient and that it is being received by him or her on a soul level—or even a conscious level, if that is your intention. If you wish, send light or a spoken or sung tone with your message as you let it go.

Alternatively, use the space to write out any wishes for light and love you may be sending out to others (some traditions, of course, call these prayers). Again, close the journal and know they are on their way.

MEDITATION

DAILY EXPERIENCE

PSYCHIC WORK

MEDITATION

DAILY EXPERIENCE

PSYCHIC WORK

"Here is an exercise in the basic technique of creative visualization:

"First, think of something you would like. For this exercise choose something simple, that you can easily imagine attaining. It might be an object you would like to have, an event which you would like to happen, a situation in which you'd like to find yourself, or some circumstance in your life which you'd like to improve.

"Get in a comfortable position, either sitting or lying down, in a quiet place where you won't be disturbed. Relax your body completely. Starting from your toes and moving up to your scalp, think of relaxing each muscle in your body in turn, letting all tension flow out of your body. Breathe deeply and slowly, from your belly. Count down slowly from 10 to 1, feeling yourself getting more deeply relaxed with each count.

"When you feel deeply relaxed, start to imagine the thing you want exactly as you would like it. If it is an object, imagine yourself with the object, using it, admiring it, enjoying it, showing it to friends. If it is a situation or event, imagine yourself there and everything happening just as you want it to. You may imagine what people are saying, or any details that make it more real to you.

"You may take a relatively short time or quite a few minutes to imagine this—whatever feels best to you. Have fun with it. It should be a thoroughly enjoyable experience, like a child daydreaming about what he wants for his birthday.

"Now keeping the idea or image still in your mind, mentally make some very positive affirmative statements to yourself. . . .

"Always end your visualization with the firm statement to yourself 'This, or something better, now manifests for me in totally satisfying and harmonious ways, for the highest good of all concerned.'"

Shakti Gawain,
Creative Visualization

Take a moment to review this section of your *Inner Voyager*. Use the space below to note any new personal patterns and symbols.

_____

_____

_____

_____

_____

Now go back to Inner Reviews 1, 2, and 3, and your answers to the exercise above. Pinpoint the three strongest types of intuitive experiences you have had through the experience of personal patterns and symbols or during psychic work. These will be the intuitive experiences you have most frequently or intensely that, in retrospect, have given you the best information about your own life during this cycle. Write these three types of experience below.

_____

_____

_____

_____

_____

_____

_____

_____

_____

_____

_____

_____

_____

These types of intuitive experiences are your current *intuitive strengths*. There is a good chance that by tuning in to these strong intuitive currents you can get a great deal of information when you need it. Now go back and look for the *medium* in which they were expressed to you: Was it in a dream, or just before you fell asleep? Through meditation? In the course of a tarot reading? After using the *I Ching*? While you were washing the dishes, mowing the lawn, waiting on line, or exercising? During a session with your bodyworker or intuitive counselor?

_____

_____

_____

_____

_____

_____

_____

_____

_____

_____

_____

_____

Date: _____

Suggestion: During the next month, take advantage of these mediums and your intuitive strengths to access your inner guidance when you need to make decisions or require additional information about a person, place, or experience. Combine them. Try tuning in to intuitive images or feelings when you're doing housework. Consult the *I Ching* right before you go to bed. Meditate unobtrusively while you're waiting for your theater date. Listen for that inner voice while you're doing a tarot reading. Reidentify your intuitive strengths and most fertile mediums whenever you sense they may be changing.

Then said a teacher, Speak to us of Teaching.

And he said:

No man can reveal to you aught but that which already lies half asleep in the dawning of your knowledge.

The teacher who walks in the shadow of the temple, among his followers, gives not of his wisdom but rather of his faith and his lovingness.

If he is indeed wise he does not bid you enter the house of his wisdom, but rather leads you to the threshold of your own mind.

The astronomer may speak to you of his understanding of space, but he cannot give you his understanding.

The musician may sing to you of the rhythm which is in all space, but he cannot give you the ear which arrests the rhythm nor the voice that echoes it.

And he who is versed in the science of numbers can tell of the regions of weight and measure, but he cannot conduct you thither.

For the vision of one man lends not its wings to another man.

And even as each one of you stands alone in God's knowledge, so must each one of you be alone in his knowledge of God and in his understanding of the earth.

Kahlil Gibran, The Prophet

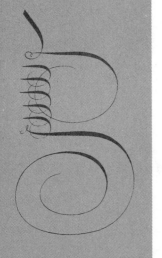

'Tis the gift to be simple
'Tis the gift to be free
'Tis the gift to find out
Where we ought to be
And when we get to the place
    just right
it will be in the valley
    of love and delight.

When true simplicity is
    gained
to bow and to bend
we shan't be ashamed
to turn, turn will be our
    delight
and by turning, turning we'll
    come out right.

☙☙☙☙

They buried my body and
    they thought I'd gone,
But I am the dance and I still
    go on. . .
They cut me down and I leap
    up high. . .
I am the life that'll never
    die. . . .

Shaker hymns

MEDITATION

DAILY EXPERIENCE

PSYCHIC WORK

Today, as you write, see each sentence as a flowing, natural step in your development: not something permanent or final but a thought or observation on its way toward expressing the Ultimate Expression of Life Itself. No matter how far you get, you'll always be on your way. And no matter how far away you feel, when you write in your *Inner Voyager* you are always dancing the eternal dance that is the source of awareness.

You can use this technique whenever you're feeling at a loss for words.

The key to using the medicine wheel is movement, the way a person moves from one direction to another. For example, a woman living in trust and innocence in the south of the medicine wheel may progress through a series of life experiences and reach a state of wisdom and strength in the north. At this point of wisdom, she has grown from a life of materialism in the south to a position of spirit in the north. The key to evolving further again is movement. Because she has gone from the south looking north for the spirit, she must now move from north in spirit looking south for substance. After manifesting substance, she must then travel back north to manifest spirit, and so on.

Lynn V. Andrews,
Star Woman

At dusk the cock announces
dawn;
At midnight, the bright sun.

Zen poem

MEDITATION

DAILY EXPERIENCE

PSYCHIC WORK

Perhaps intuitively sensing this potent effect of the symbolic, Kabbalistic adepts have also performed a specific method of meditation . . . related to the celestial Tree. . . . The room should be dark and quiet. Then, visualize a white light surrounding you with warmth and tranquility. Next, picture this light as circulating upward from the Sefirot corresponding to the systems of your body—until the light merges into the brilliant sea of the Ein Sof ("Infinite"). Briefly dwell on the image of this endless, dazzling light around you.

Thereupon, visualize this light as traveling downward, through each of the Sefirot, until it descends into the most earthbound aspects of your being—transforming with radiance your cares and worries. Feel the intensity of the light dissolving them. Chaim Vital, the sixteenth-century Safed thinker, explains:

"Think and intend to receive light from the ten spheres from that point tangential to your soul. There you intend to raise the ten spheres up to the Infinite so that from There (beyond the Sefirot) an illumination will be drawn to them—to the lowest level (of your mind and body)."

Edward Hoffman,
The Way of Splendor

*Inside the hidden nexus,
from within the sealed secret,
a zohar flashed,
shining as a mirror,
embracing two colors blended
together.
Once these two absorbed
each other, all colors
appeared:
purple, the whole spectrum of
colors, flashing, disap-
pearing.*

"Jacob's Journey," in
The Zohar, translated
by Daniel Chanan Matt

May the warp be the white light of morning,
May the weft be the red light of evening,
May the fringes be the falling rain,
May the border be the standing rainbow.
Thus weave for us a garment of brightness.

Tewa Indians,
"Song of the Sky Loom"

MEDITATION

DAILY EXPERIENCE

PSYCHIC WORK

There have been times when I am aware of incredibly powerful energy flows within my body during trances. I can see the color of the energy as it flows. I can see it spark as it comes off the palms of my hands. It is as if a part of me is above the physical self, still a part of the whole, but I am a separate consciousness observing another part of myself. Once I remember seeing a brilliant blue light coming off the ends of my fingers and orange lights covering the palms of my hands. My hands became hot, and I watched the energy flowing all through my body in different colors. It was indescribably beautiful—running over my skin, coming off my feet, off my toes, and the ends of my fingers. Most of the colors were green and blue, with some purple and orange cascading over my hands.

Sheila Petersen-Lowary,
The Fifth Dimension

"Hold your hands about one foot from your eyes against a dark background or a white wall in shadow. Spread your fingers apart and touch your left-hand fingertips against your right. Now, concentrate on visualizing energy flowing into your fingers. Hold them there together for a minute, then draw them apart, keeping your eyes focused on the gradually widening space between them. You will see minute radiations of energy issuing from your fingertips, bridging the gap between your two hands.

"It may help if you rub your hands vigorously together before you do this exercise. Alternatively, try this as a warm-up. Hold your hands close together . . . and imagine the space between them filling with energy. Then move them slowly together and apart again in a gentle pulsing movement. As the energy builds, you may sense a tingling in the palms of your hands, and eventually this charge may become so strong that you have the impression you are squeezing an invisible sponge. Now put your fingertips together and look for the auric radiation the same way as before."

Jonathan Cainer
and Carl Rider,
The Psychic Explorer

IRIS. This ancient divinity was the daughter of Thaumas and Electra. Messenger, servant, and even the confidante of Hera, she took pains to obey even the most insignificant of orders from her mistress. She symbolizes the rainbow, the bridge between heaven and earth, between the gods and men, that she uses in her travels, in the form of a winged young woman, holding in one hand the wand of a herald.

Larousse Greek and Roman Mythology

TEMPERANCE

Rainbows are the closest manifestations of pure white light that can be witnessed on the physical plane. . . . As light enters the physical plane, it expresses itself in an infinite number of ways. In reality, everything is the play of that light and color upon itself. Rainbows are a most special symbol of the light in panoramic color and multifaceted forms. They are representative of the entire creation. When rainbows are seen after rainstorms, it is a reminder of hope and renewed life. The rainbow unites and integrates the heavens with the earth, and upon that ray life can be born anew. . . .

The rainbows found in crystals dance delightfully as the crystals are turned and played with in the light. Rainbow Crystals can teach us how to be multifaceted in our own unique expression of light while still remaining pure and colorfully conscious in all aspects of living. . . . In Rainbow Crystal meditations, the human awareness can travel the rainbow ray all the way back to the source of pure light, the great central sun. . . . When the human soul aligns with this cosmic force, reality takes on a new dimension and one becomes personally empowered.

Katrina Raphaell,
Crystal Enlightenment,
Aurora Press

It's important at this time that people open themselves secondly to discernment, not just the heart but the mind as well. In your world there's such a criticism of thinking . . . Yes, we would agree, if that means thinking alone. . . . We would suggest here that feeling, alone . . . can turn you into a spent dandelion—fluff floating in the cosmic breeze of reality, with no grounding, no understanding. No, we would suggest that what you're here to do is combine them to create a whole that is greater, a whole that is your intuition, a whole that is your discernment, a whole that is your ability, your inner guidance. . . . And then bring these raw ingredients together to create a whole, to create a world that is your intuition, that is your creativity, that is your discernment at this particular time.

Lazaris, in The Channeling Process, *by Jon Klimo*

Everything an Indian does is in a circle, and that is because the power of the world works in circles, and everything tries to be round. In the old days when we were a strong and happy people, all our power came to us from the sacred hoop of the nation, and so long as the hoop was unbroken the people flourished. . . .

Even the seasons form a great circle in their changing, and always come back again to where they were. The life of a man is a circle from childhood to childhood and so it is in everything where power moves. Our tepees were round like the nests of birds, and these were always set in a circle, the nation's hoop.

Black Elk Speaks, *as told through John G. Neihardt*

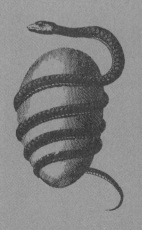

"In the beginning this world was merely nonbeing," we read in a sacred work of the Hindus; "It was existent. It developed. It turned into an egg. It lay for the period of a year. It was split asunder. One of the two eggshell parts became silver, one gold. That which was of silver is the earth. That which was of gold is the sky. What was the outer membrane is the mountains. What was the inner membrane is cloud and mist. What were the veins are the rivers. What was the fluid within is the ocean. Now, what was born therefrom is yonder sun."

Joseph Campbell, The Hero with a Thousand Faces

Look for any patterns and symbols discovered in previous Inner Reviews that you could not relate to a specific event in your daily experience. Check through the later entries to see if you can connect them with something that has happened more recently.

Review your recent entries for new patterns, symbols, and mediums. Note them here.

_____

_____

_____

_____

_____

_____

_____

_____

_____

_____

_____

_____

_____

_____

Date:

There is a space for you in *Inner Voyager* to compile a glossary of all your own personal patterns and symbols. Look for the Patterns and Symbols page in Inner Resources at the back of the book. Note there each of your personal symbols in the first column and a description of what it usually means to you in the second. If you like, use the quadrants for different kinds of symbols and patterns. For example, each could hold symbols you perceive with a different sense, or perhaps each could be reserved for those associated with a particular form of psychic work.

If you're a little hesitant about the meaning of the symbols, get hold of any thorough volume on the interpretation of symbols and images; there are several on dreams, for instance. Try a more psychically oriented one if you want to work things out against an "objective," universal ruler, or a psychoanalytic one if you feel your interpretations are already very universal and you would like to balance them using the concept of inner psyche as arbiter. Compare your interpretations with the ones in the book. The odds are they will not be exactly the same. Explain to yourself exactly how yours differ from those in the book. Use the space below as a work sheet.

[Buddha said,] "They keep misquoting me as saying that nature is unsavory; or that the point of earth life is to get over it, like a disease. And then they rant about annihilating desire, and I never said a thing like that."

Hera turned into the Virgin and said, "I probably understand humans better than any of you, and my miraculous conception told the whole tale. They just don't trust nature. They don't like the death part and they've never been able to see beyond it, really; it obsesses them. All of nature shouts of new births, yet humans have the greatest difficulty imagining any divinity in nature. I don't understand how they can be that way, but they are." . . .

"It's time for our 'nightly check,' " came the unspoken, on-the-other-side-of-silence, multimillion thought. And each divine awareness turned its attention toward the earth, seeing it and all of its parts, down to the tiniest particle; merging with the mountains, sky, seas; rushing gloriously into each living thing, exulting in the cozy preciseness of earth time.

The gods dived exuberantly into the earth minus images: growing up as trees in a million backyards, as fish in the oceans, as people and insects and animals. . . . And the gods continued to give life form, and substance to the earth.

Jane Roberts,
The Further Education
of Oversoul Seven

MEDITATION

DAILY EXPERIENCE

PSYCHIC WORK

Sky moving
as they sang
spirits sang of salmon

Sky waving
up and down
spirits singing

I was drowning
in the basin
the place of power
for curing

Spirits tossed
eagle down
to the surface
I rose singing

He pulled me out
the one who saves
those struck
by spirit power

I gazed deep
into the face
that gave me power
as a shaman

He stood up
in the center
in the center
of power

Spirit standing
in the place
of petrified
power

Sky moving
as they sang
spirits sang of salmon

Sky waving
up and down
spirits singing

Sikwalxlelix,
Bella Coola shamaness, in
Dreamtime & Inner Space,
by Holger Kalweit

The energy characteristics of the Earth's electromagnetic, gravitational, and subtle energetic fields are not homogenous, but vary with geographical location. . . . The presence of large mineral deposits, such as quartz, and of underground flowing streams, can also affect the electromagnetic fields in the overlying regions. There is evidence to suggest that the Earth has its own meridian system made up of a planetary gridwork of subtle energy channels called ley lines. Just as metals can conduct subtle-energies, . . . so can man-made metallic building structures conduct these energies, thus changing the pattern of energetic flow.

Richard Gerber, M.D.,
Vibrational Medicine

"I was driving across country, tired of the freeways and thought I'd take a short, scenic, side trip. I got off I-17, took 179 toward Sedona. When I saw Bell Rock I burst into tears. I pulled off the road, walked to the base of that great monolith, fell down, hugged the rocks, and kissed the earth. I knew I was home!"

Gayle Johansen, M.A., and
Shinan Naom Barlay, Ph.D.,
The Sedona Vortex
Experience

You yourself have known and used power spots on the earth, also known as power vortexes, whether or not you have been aware of doing so. When you were a child, was there a corner of a park that felt great to be in, or the shade of a very old and mighty tree? You may still have such a place today. If you don't, there is probably one nearby.

Take a walk, or get in the car and look around. A body of running water like a stream or river is great for cleansing and for sensing the future. Let your awareness travel down the current as you concentrate on how the future of an important issue will develop. The right steep hill, mountain, skyscraper, or even mighty tree can be a good tool for recharging your optimism and energy when you're feeling low. And a canyon, valley, or cave is a choice power spot for gaining insight about yourself, your path, dream interpretation, or past lives, and also for writing in your *Inner Voyager.* Keep in mind that power spots that combine some of the earth's features also combine their effects on awareness.

Once you've found your power spots, spend time and meditate in them. Get to know them. Make notes about their essences and effects on your awarenesses and moods. Know where to go for extra support when you do inner work.

Read aloud Sikwalxlelix's power song (turn back two pages). Feel how the rhythms spin and flow like the current of a river gaining force. Hear the strong, full current of repeating sounds giving that rhythm substance and force. This song is a shaman's power song. You too can have a power song. Try writing a song about the place of power you have identified as your own on the preceding page. You can start, if you like, by writing a phrase that describes your power place and how you feel about it. The phrase can be grammatical, or it can be just a few words that describe the place. The phrase can even be made up of sounds and syllables in a language all your own.

Once you have a phrase you are happy with, build other like phrases (in sound, length, rhythm) around it. Keep your song simple and brief, if you like. Keep repeating it out loud to see if the rhythms are right, adapting and experimenting until it expresses you perfectly. Chant or sing your song whenever you are away from your place and want to affirm your own awakening power. Don't tell anyone else what it is. It's a private secret for you alone.

Virginia Beach, the information said, was the place to build. It gave reasons: Edgar Cayce should live near large bodies of water. It was best for his health and for his psychic abilities. It was also best for psychic work of any kind to be carried on near water. It was best that people, coming for readings, travel over water to get them. It would put them in the right vibration and help them to cooperate in the "experiment." The attitude of the person asking for the reading was of great importance.

Thomas Sugrue,
There Is a River

No matter what you are doing, keep the undercurrent of happiness, the secret river of joy, flowing beneath the sands of your various thoughts and the rocky soil of your hard trials. Learn to be secretly happy within your heart in spite of all circumstances.

Paramahansa Yogananda

The wood, clearly the work of nature not of man, was a wonderful mixture of every sort of tree. There were oaks and ashes and beeches and larches and firs and wild cherries and some of the largest yews Edward had ever seen. It was an old wood. The old tall trees made a labyrinth of colonnades and archways and vaulted halls and domed chambers, and if Edward had not entrusted himself to the little path he would soon have been lost. Some birds were singing, nearby a blackbird and a loud wren. Distant rooks cawed sadly. Occasionally, some sunlight fell upon the path, which was dry and brown, crisscrossed with ridgy tree roots, almost like steps, and scattered with the mysterious dried-up fruits of various trees fashioned into little brown toys and emblems, which crackled pleasantly underfoot. All round about the antique carpet of fallen leaves stretched far away. The path was steeper now and there was a larger light ahead. Edward began to walk faster and after a minute or two he came to a place.

Of course the wood was full of places, celebrations and juxtapositions, mossy alcoves, primroses showing off in the dead bracken, circlets of greenery where the sun managed to shine, long fallen trees as clean as bones. But now Edward, coming out into a larger clearing, stopped as one who, exploring the palace, accidentally opens the door of the chapel. The elongated oval sward, though shorter, not two hundred yard in length, curiously reminded Edward of the stadium at Delphi. He shivered.

Iris Murdoch,
The Good Apprentice

Cosmologically, the World Tree rises at the center of the earth, the place of earth's "umbilicus," and its upper branches touch the place of Bai Uglan. . . . The Tree connects the three cosmic regions. . . . It represents the universe in continual regeneration, the inexhaustible spring of cosmic life, the paramount reservoir of the sacred. . . . In a number of archaic traditions the Cosmic Tree . . . is related to the ideas of creation, fecundity, and initiations, and finally to the idea of absolute reality and immortality. . . . The Cosmic Tree always presents itself as the very reservoir of life and the master of destinies.

Mircea Eliade,
Shamanism: Archaic
Techniques of Ecstasy

I went to the woods because I wished to live deliberately, to confront only the essential facts of life, and see if I could not learn what it had to teach, and not, when I came to die, discover that I had not lived. . . . I wanted to live deep and suck out all the marrow of life, to live so sturdily and Spartan-like as to put to rout all that was not life, to cut a broad swath and shave close, to drive life into a corner, and reduce it to its lowest terms.

Henry David Thoreau,
Walden

The Higher Self, as expressed through the causal body, is the gestalt consciousness of all that the soul has learned and experienced throughout its many lifetimes upon the physical plane. *The causal body might be viewed as a tree trunk of a large oak tree with many branches. Each of the branches of the tree represents a different personality and life experience of the soul. Imagine that a tremendous flood of water has immersed the tree so that only its uppermost branches can be seen poking through the water. To the ordinary consciousness, it would seem that each branch above the water is a separate plant, but beneath the water and beyond the perspective of the superficial observer, each branch is an outgrowth and expression of a common trunk and nurturing root system.*

Richard Gerber, M.D.,
Vibrational Medicine

MEDITATION

DAILY EXPERIENCE

PSYCHIC WORK

Historically, these [ten primordial energies] have been
depicted in various diagrams,
the most favored being the
Tree of Life. . . .

Kabbalists have literally
written volumes about this
celestial Tree. It is worth
noting that its roots are seen
to lie in the most transcendent reaches beyond our comprehension. With the
appearance of each Sefira in
the cosmos, some of the divine energy was diluted, until
the world around us was
created. But link by link, the
Kabbalists stress, we are in-
separably connected to the
most hidden and exalted dimensions of being. . . . The
powers of the divine Sefirot
also flow within each of us.

Edward Hoffman,
The Way of Splendor

Think of yourself as a mountain climber of the mind. Let the flaming spirit within you mark the path as you go. You have nothing to fear, and nothing of true value to lose.

LaUna Huffines,
Bridge of Light

You look at that mountain, that mountain has a spirit, that mountain has holiness. There's a quiet there and yet there's a fervor there. And if you've ever seen clouds there you see that mountain like a hand grasping those clouds.
   There's life up there. That's why it's sacred.

The Indian Peoples
of the Southwest, in
Our Voices, Our Land

The places where you live and work also have power spots. Use the same technique discussed earlier to sense the power spots or vortexes in these areas, too. See if they coincide with the places you spend the most time (your work, sleeping, and inner work areas). Do the places where you perform most of your activities coincide with the spots that feel best for them? If not, try writing in your *Inner Voyager*, meditating, or doing psychic work in the places you have discovered. Note the results. Do a little rearranging, if you feel like it. And use those results to support your intuitive and spiritual explorations.

MEDITATION

DAILY EXPERIENCE

PSYCHIC WORK

The southeast is the source of illumination, life and renewal. Its color is white, and its totem is the golden eagle, who—because it flies so high and is so powerful and sharp eyed—is considered a principal intermediary between the Above Beings and humans.

Thomas E. Mails,
Secret Native American
Indian Pathways

Choose a major issue in your life that you suspect might benefit from a little inner review of its own: for example, intimacy, love, trust, prosperity, empowerment, control—or lack of it— resentment, humor, healing, or energy level.

_____

_____

_____

_____

_____

Peruse your Daily Experience entries in the previous _Inner Voyager_ cycles (go back as far as you like) and pick out the entries that pertain to this issue, either directly or indirectly. Now look over the Meditation and Psychic Work entries close to these Daily Experience entries. Is there a connection? An inflection to your meditation or something in your intuitive practice that reflects your larger challenge? If so, write about it here.

_____

_____

_____

_____

_____

_____

_____

_____

_____

_____

_____

_____

_____

_____

_____

_____

_____

_____

_____

_____

_____

_____

_____

_____

_____

_____

_____

_____

_____

_____

_____

_____

_____

_____

Date: _____

Suggestion: Next cycle, try shifting the quality of your meditation and psychic work away from the patterns you have just identified. Create a new pattern to substitute when the old ones come up. A simple example: If your issue is loneliness and you have found that your meditations seem too self-centered, send love and light out to others when that feeling comes up. Do not feel frustrated if your problem and its solution are not as simple as this. Usually they aren't. Instead, work intuitively to find the right substitute and experiment with it, refining as necessary. End result: The shift in your intuitive work will gently make changes in your daily experience and hence in your major life issue. It's the metaphysical theorem "The part reflects the whole" in action.

Reminder: Update your list of Patterns and Symbols in Inner Resources with this cycle's additions.

A king had built a glorious palace full of corridors and partitions, but he himself lived in the innermost room. When the palace was completed and his servants came to pay him homage, they found that they could not approach the king because of the devious maze. While they stood and wondered, the king's son came and showed them that those were not real partitions, but only magical illusions, and that the king, in truth, was easily accessible. Push forward bravely and you shall find no obstacle.

Baal Shem Tov

*Morning is when I am awake
and there is a dawn in me.*

Henry David Thoreau,
Walden

*Rest at pale evening . . .
A tall slim tree . . .
Night coming tenderly
Black like me.*

Langston Hughes,
"Dream Variations"

*Time cools, time clarifies; no
mood can be maintained
quite unaltered through the
course of hours.*

Thomas Mann,
The Magic Mountain

Every time of day has its own unique characteristics in terms of energy and mood, and each of these, in turn, has a unique effect on each of us. Some people meditate best in the morning and write with greatest vigor in the evening. Others find the inverse is the case. Doing psychic work at noon in a sunny country field may support you differently than doing the same work at sunset in a chapel. Doing deep intuitive work with a counselor on a challenging situation or relationship could affect you differently depending on whether you do the work in the late afternoon or before you go to sleep.

Experiment with your different intuitive activities at different times of day. Note and record, for instance, what happens when you meditate in the morning, evening, and afternoon, and if there is a difference in what you experience at different times of day. See if bodywork has a more profound effect when you schedule a session at a particular time of day. (For some activities and people, it also may make no difference at all.) If you like, keep experimenting until you find patterns. Know this information is available to you here and that you can use time as a tool to shape and support your growth.

THE
FOOL

I have a series of emotions that I feel within myself, and it's my process for connecting with her personality. . . . And so I experience that. At the point that I get to within my own being with peace, I experience almost like a tumbling. It's like I'm tumbling somewhere, and I never know where I'm tumbling to, but again, it's not an uncomfortable feeling. It's a very comfortable feeling. In fact it feels like beautiful. It's like you're free-floating, free falling. . . just in space, but it is down too, but it's like there's no bottom, you know, there's no top, there's no sides, there's no bottom, it just is.

C.M., trance channel, in
The Channeling Process,
by Margo Chandley, Ph.D.

Alice started to her feet, for it flashed across her mind that she had never before seen a rabbit with either a waist-coat-pocket, or a watch to take out of it, and, burning with curiosity, she ran across the field after it, and was just in time to see it pop down a large rabbit-hole under the hedge.

In another moment down went Alice after it, never once considering how in the world she was to get out again.

The rabbit-hole went straight on like a tunnel for some way, and then dipped suddenly down, so suddenly that Alice had not a moment to think about stopping herself before she found herself falling down what seemed to be a very deep well.

Either the well was very deep, or she fell very slowly, for she had plenty of time as she went down to look about her, and to wonder what was going to happen next.

Lewis Carroll,
Alice's Adventures in
Wonderland

MEDITATION

DAILY EXPERIENCE

PSYCHIC WORK

Clarity! That clarity of mind, which is so hard to obtain, dispels fear, but also blinds. It forces the man never to doubt himself. It gives him the assurance he can do anything he pleases, for he sees clearly into everything. And he is courageous because he is clear, and he stops at nothing because he is clear. But all that is a mistake; it is like something incomplete. If the man yields to this make-believe power, he has succumbed. . . . He must defy his clarity and use it only to see, and wait patiently and measure carefully before taking new steps; he must think, above all, that his clarity is almost a mistake. And a moment will come when he will understand that his clarity was only a point before his eyes. And thus . . . he . . . will arrive at a position where nothing can harm him anymore. This will not be a mistake. It will not be only a point before his eyes. It will be true power.

Carlos Castaneda,
The Teachings of Don Juan

Until that moment Vetch had watched him with an anxious dread, for he was not sure what had happened there in the dark land. He did not know if this was Ged in the boat with him, and his hand had been for hours ready to the anchor, to stave in the boat's planking and sink her there in midsea, rather than carry back to the harbors of Earthsea the evil thing that he feared might have taken Ged's look and form. Now when he saw his friend and heard him speak, his doubt vanished. And he began to see the truth, that Ged had neither lost nor won but, naming the shadow of his death with his own name, had made himself whole: a man: who, knowing his whole true self, cannot be used or possessed by any power other than himself, and whose life therefore is lived for life's sake and never in the service of ruin, or pain, or hatred, or the dark. In the Creation of Ea, which is the oldest song, it is said, "Only in silence the word, only in dark the light, only in dying life: bright the hawk's flight on the empty sky." That song Vetch sang aloud now as he held the boat westward, going before the cold wind of the winter night that blew at their backs from the vastness of the Open Sea.

Ursula K. Le Guin,
A Wizard of Earthsea

And Jacob was left alone; and a man wrestled with him until the breaking of the day. When the man saw that he did not prevail against Jacob, he touched the hollow of his thigh; and Jacob's thigh was put out of joint as he wrestled with him. Then he said, "Let me go, for the day is breaking." But Jacob said, "I will not let you go, unless you bless me." And he said to him, "What is your name?" And he said, "Jacob." Then he said, "Your name shall no more be called Jacob, but Israel, for you have striven with God and with men, and have prevailed." Then Jacob asked him, "Tell me, I pray, your name." But he said, "Why is it that you ask my name?" And there he blessed him. So Jacob called the name of the place Peniel, saying, "For I have seen God face to face, and yet my life is preserved."

Genesis 32.24-30

In your meditation, visualize your own personal dark angel, the part of yourself and aspect of universal energy we all confront to gain power and freedom. What does your dark angel look like? Is its energy masculine or feminine? Is your dark angel human in aspect, animal, a combination? Or is its aspect more abstract? Does it speak to you? What else, if anything, must you learn about it to be "blessed" with integration?

I see a pattern. But my imagination cannot picture the maker of that pattern. I see the clock. But I cannot envisage the clockmaker. The human mind is unable to conceive of the four dimensions. How can it conceive of a God, before whom a thousand years and a thousand dimensions are as one?

Albert Einstein,
Cosmic Religion

All matter, both physical and subtle, has frequency. Matter of different frequencies can coexist in the same space, just as energies of different frequencies (i.e. radio and TV) can exist nondestructively in the same space.

Richard Gerber, M.D.,
Vibrational Medicine

Regarding Einstein as a kind of twentieth-century Kabbalist par excellence, some theoretical physicists by formal training suggest that the Kabbalistic scheme of the Sefirot and the four worlds may be perfectly possible. Such scientists have boldly suggested that each of the four universes described in the Kabbalah may indeed exist, vibrating at differing rates of speed, interpenetrating everywhere at the same time. Other scientists have theorized that each universe may fluctuate in its vibrations so that when one is active and "on," the others lie dormant or "off." Yet, because our clocks and all else in our own dimension would "wink" on/off together, we would not observe any measurable gap in its continuity. Though such ideas may seem the sole province of science fiction, a growing number of physicists with impeccable academic credentials are taking them quite seriously indeed. In fact, even a casual perusing of current publications in the field reveals that contemporary researchers are attempting to grapple like mystics with the fundamental attributes of time and matter.

Edward Hoffman,
The Way of Splendor

And stepping westward
seemed to be
A kind of heavenly destiny.

William Wordsworth,
"Stepping Westward"

The northwest is the place of introspection, perfection, beauty, and harvest. Its color is yellow, and its totem is the bear spirit.

Thomas E. Mails,
Secret Native American
Pathways

Have in your hold the great image
And the empire will come to you.

Lao Tzu, Tao Te Ching

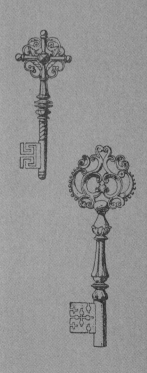

Use this space to write down your own personal favorite visualizations for meditation, personal empowerment, or psychic work. Or, if you like, close your eyes and visualize your greatest goal achieved. Render each detail of your vision in loving, colorful detail. Take as much time as you like to really look at your vision realized and to know that on some level it already has been realized. Then use this space and the rest of this entry to record every single detail so that you can look at it whenever you like.

Crystal healing is a progressive art, one that has the potential to create complete healing, inclusive of the mental, emotional, physical, and spiritual bodies. Practicing crystal healing is an opportunity to let go and let God. It is the time when the heart listens to the messages of the soul, a time to plunge deeply into trust in the inner self. Crystal healing is dedicated to the highest energies of light and color as they act upon the subtle levels of the human being. When this energy interaction takes place, the deepest essence of a person can be accessed. It then becomes possible to see why we have created the realities that we have in our lives. When we understand why we have attracted our circumstances and what the invaluable spiritual lessons are inherent in our life's events, we can then take complete responsibility for ourselves and create our lives the way we choose. Peace and personal empowerment are the natural way of being to one who is in harmony with the self and understands the sometimes hidden purpose behind why events happen in life the way that they do. It is then no longer necessary to play the role of victim, of the controlled, the powerless, and the prisoner of life.

Katrina Raphaell,
Crystal Healing,
Aurora Press

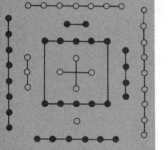

MEDITATION

DAILY EXPERIENCE

PSYCHIC WORK

A Zen teacher in London had a friend with a particularly vexing problem. Jana had been seduced by her therapist, a world-renowned man who'd promised to marry her. At this point their child was eighteen months old and she was still single. As a foreign national she had immigration difficulties in Great Britain. Though she could have reported her live-in lover and former therapist to the appropriate professional bodies, she refused, always saying, "The Universe will take care of it."

To this the Zen teacher stated, "She doesn't realize she's part of the Universe."

When the situation is yours, you are the one who has to deal with it or it's very unlikely to be taken care of.

Jana purchased a large Arkansas clear quartz crystal which she placed on the nightstand by her bed. The crystal acted as a receptacle for the emotional grip the relationship had over her. At night her thoughts were cleared, and the hold her lover had on her was broken. Within a few weeks she threatened him with public exposure and he married her long enough to legitimize their child and grant her permanent resident status in England. He also provided the financial support he had been reneging on during the time she'd been unable to take action.

If you don't get into your shadow side, you won't be able to get into your saint either. Jana needed to let her power out, but she'd been afraid to see her own shadow.

Laeh Maggie Garfield,
Sound Medicine

I want to emphasize . . . the difference between wishing, which is passive, and hope, which is active. Hoping means seeing that the outcome you want is possible, and then working for it. Wishing means just sitting there, waiting for a miracle to happen out of the blue. Jung said, "Every problem, therefore, brings the possibility of a widening of consciousness, but also the necessity of saying goodbye to the childlike unconsciousness and trust in nature," a process he likened to leaving the Garden of Eden. I encourage patients to have faith in God but not to expect Him to do all the work.

Bernie S. Siegel, M.D., Love, Medicine & Miracles

What general observations can you make about the way you developed your psychic skills this cycle, and about your experiences in general? Do you associate them with a specific color, mood, peak experience, or challenge? Think of a peak experience and an especially challenging situation. Is there a connection between them?

Which form of psychic work or meditation do you use least often? Which medium seems most challenging to you on a regular basis? Review as many cycles as you like. Write your results below.

_____

_____

_____

_____

_____

_____

_____

_____

_____

_____

_____

_____

_____

_____

_____

_____

Date: _____

Often, your seemingly least-developed intuitive sense is the one that is most instinctive and through which you are likely to receive particularly "deep" messages, such as instinctive hunches that keep you from harm's door or communications about others passing.

Suggestion: This cycle, make a point of "flexing" this muscle. Consciously use it _first_ to get guidance and only then use your most fluent skill. Compare the results in terms of both strength of impression and accuracy. Remember to update your list of Patterns and Symbols.

MEDITATION

DAILY EXPERIENCE

PSYCHIC WORK

*Speech is civilization itself.
The word, even the most
contradictory word, preserves
contact—it is silence which
isolates.*

Thomas Mann,
The Magic Mountain

A woman who required money, and who knew the spiritual law of opulence, was thrown continually in a business-way, with a man who made her feel very poor. He talked lack and limitation and she commenced to catch his poverty thoughts, so she disliked him, and blamed him for her failure. She knew in order to demonstrate her supply [of opulence], she must first feel that she had received—a feeling of opulence must precede its manifestation.

It dawned upon her, one day, that she was resisting the situation, and seeing two powers instead of one. So she blessed the man and baptized the situation "Success"! She affirmed, "As there is only one power, God, this man is here for my good and my prosperity" (just what he did not seem to be there for). Soon after that she met, through this man, a woman who gave her for a service rendered, several thousand dollars, and the man moved to a distant city, and faded harmoniously from her life. Make the statement, "Every man is a golden link in the chain of my good," for all men are God in manifestation, awaiting the opportunity given by man, himself, to serve the divine plan of his life.

"Bless your enemy, and you rob him of his ammunition." His arrows will be transmuted into blessings.

Florence Scovel Shinn,
The Game of Life

Even a single figure, such as Artemis the lunar goddess, or Hermes the trickster god, cannot be disinterred from the stories in which it is embedded. Myth contains motion, and is not static. It describes processes and movements, as well as qualities. A zodiacal sign, seen through mythic eyes, is also a dynamic story, rather than one set of character traits or one mode of behaviour. Each sign contains its own conflicts, ambivalences, dualities, motives, lacks, longings, collisions and resolutions between characters. It is my experience that when these dynamic figures move within a personality— and their movements can be seen most clearly in dreams and in astrological progressions and transits—they reflect movement between different parts of the psyche. If we exteriorize our myths, which all of us do at different times in life, then we draw others into our lives to take up one role or another, and we identify unconsciously with one or another figure in the story. In this way, the figures of myth are the active and dynamic aspect of our fate, the daimones, and we draw the outer world into our own myths at the points where the outer world's myths touch our own. Thus we, as the vessels for myth, create our fate.

Liz Greene,
The Astrology of Fate

Calvin nodded again. . . .
"You mean you're comparing
our lives to a sonnet? A strict
form, but freedom within it?"
"Yes," Mrs. Whatsit said.
"You're given the form, but
you have to write the sonnet
yourself. What you say is
completely up to you."

Madeleine L'Engle,
A Wrinkle in Time

MEDITATION

DAILY EXPERIENCE

PSYCHIC WORK

Many fiction writers and dramatists discover—sometimes to their delight and other times to their dismay—that events they described in their imaginative stories were prophetic. You, too, can tap into your own intuitive storytelling ability to receive guidance about your life and the lives of others.

Start by focusing through meditation. Then tune into a situation that you want to know more about. It could be one in your own life or one involving other people. Now visualize an empty room or a natural setting and see all the characters involved in this setting. What do they say to each other? Are some talkative and others silent? Or are they all silent?

Write it down. You can write a little fictional scene with description or lines of dialogue and stage directions like a play or screenplay.

Now, focusing on the characters and their words, move your awareness forward in time and discover what happens to them next. Do some of your characters begin to move around? Do others sit still and ignore the first group? Do they leave this setting for another scenario? What happens there? And then what? Develop the story until it seems to reach a point of resolution. If you like, use any of the "getting unstuck" techniques in the Introduction to move the story along.

Leave the finished story alone for a while and then go back to it. Let at least a morning, afternoon, or evening pass before you take a look. What does the finished story tell you about the situation in question? Write that down, too.

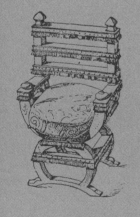

All the world's a stage,
And all the men and women
merely players.

William Shakespeare,
As You Like It, Act II

Metaphorical language, parabolic language, does not take us out of everyday reality but drives us more deeply into it, de-forming our usual apprehensions in such a way that we see that reality in a new way. The second "logic" like all new meaning is a deepening of reality, not an escape from it into a never-never land. What we see . . . is not a new reality but the same reality in a new perspective. The mundane world is transmuted; no new world is created. . . . The story is the screen or "smoked glass" through which we perceive the new logic of grace.

Sallie TeSelle,
Speaking in Parables

Find the dynamic myths in your life. To gain some light on bewildering situations, use the Myths and Archetypes section in Inner Resources or the myth cluster of your choice (or your favorite book on mythology or archetypes). "Cast" people you know as different characters. Write down the casting on the page. You might want to cast them as different astrological planetary aspects, or as reflections of the different energy centers interacting within you, or as your different numerological aspects, or as personifications of images from tarot, or even your favorite spiritual writers and role models.

Next, put all the characters in a room. How do they interact? What do they say to each other? How do your characters feel? What happens? How does everything play out? Can you use this story to get you through the situation in question? Does it show you how to avoid something unpleasant? Or how to appreciate something wonderful you might have overlooked? This playful technique can be the source of both delight and insight.

The Chautauquas were pushed aside by faster-paced radio, movies and TV, and it seems to me the change was not entirely an improvement. Perhaps because of these changes the stream of national consciousness moves faster now, and is broader, but it seems to run less deep. The old channels cannot contain it and in its search for new ones there seems to be growing havoc and destruction along its banks. . . . I would like not to cut any new channels of consciousness but simply dig deeper into old ones that have become silted in with the debris of thoughts grown stale and platitudes too often repeated. "What's new?" is an interesting and broadening eternal question, but one which, if pursued exclusively, results only in an endless parade of trivia and fashion, the silt of tomorrow. I would like, instead, to be concerned with the question "What is best?"

Robert M. Pirsig,
Zen and the Art of
Motorcycle Maintenance

MEDITATION

DAILY EXPERIENCE

PSYCHIC WORK

"Here is an exercise that can be done anywhere, at any time, to decrystallize fear:

"Place yourself in a meditative state by simply taking in a series of long breaths. Breathe in slowly and exhale slowly, drawing in light with each breath and exhaling thoughts and agitation from the body. Ask your body where it is holding fear. Simply ask the question, continue breathing deeply, and notice when you feel a sensation in some part of your body or hear the answer. Trust any sensation or feeling you get and go right to that place. Allow your consciousness to rest there and feel yourself moving deeply into the area, using all your perceptive capacities to connect with this area. How does the fear look or smell or feel? What colors do you see there? Then ask the body what color it needs to dissolve the fear. Accept the first color you see or hear or feel. Draw that color into the body with your breath and allow it to fill up completely the area with the stored fear. Keep drawing it into you until the body can receive not another drop. As you feel the color filling the area, simply be aware that it is absorbing and dissolving all the fear within you. You will know when it is enough. You will feel differently inside yourself— to some people it feels peaceful and lifting, to others it is a more active, ecstatic state. However you perceive it, when you feel the change, just open your eyes and go on. You can use this exercise in an anxious moment on the telephone or a fearful encounter. What is fascinating about this is that when you use the color to dissolve the fear, you actually dissolve the cause simultaneously. Each is linked to the other through the magnetic attraction. *When we change the energy, we change the reality.*"

Chris Griscom,
Time Is an Illusion

Many people have cited examples of past life memories
from dreams. Some of those
individuals, who have recurring dreams, may not think to
acknowledge the possibility
that glimpses of past lives may
be trying to filter through for
an important reason. There
are other examples of fragmentary information that
comes on a conscious level
and seems to have no meaning at all. Yet later on, at
an unexpected moment, a
chance meeting or a view of a
particular bit of scenery will
trigger more information to
complete the whole picture.

Jeanne Avery,
Astrology and
Your Past Lives

3 December

I dreamed that the storm was approaching from the sea. Huge black clouds rolling on and on, nearer and nearer. I began to close the windows on the side of the approaching storm but left open those on the other side of the house, thinking they were safe because facing the sun; the sky was still blue and clear on this side of the horizon.

"The dream is incomplete. Not much use telling you what it could mean, because it will only mislead you. I have told you that the past will come up in dreams now, as the time goes on. Ninety nine and a half per cent of the karmas will be dealt with in dreams; the remaining half per cent of course. . . ." He fell silent looking into the far distance. Into my past or into my future?

Irina Tweedie,
Daughter of Fire

Try using the close description technique when you write about dreams. Often, the close description process (writing about every detail of a single object in your dream, then widening out to treat all aspects of the dream in the same way) yields insight about the deepest matrix of your soul or some other important aspect of self-awareness.

MEDITATION

DAILY EXPERIENCE

PSYCHIC WORK

Mountains should be climbed with as little effort as possible and without desire. The reality of our own nature should determine the speed. If you become restless, speed up. If you become winded, slow down. You climb the mountain in an equilibrium between restlessness and exhaustion. Then, when you're no longer thinking ahead, each footstep isn't just a means to an end but a unique event in itself. This leaf has jagged edges. This rock looks loose. From this place the snow is less visible, even though closer. These are things you should notice, anyway. To live only for some future goal is shallow. It's the sides of the mountain which sustain life, not the top. Here's where things grow.

Robert M. Pirsig,
Zen and the Art of
Motorcycle Maintenance

My great-grandfather and my grandfathers were shamans. They sang wind songs and healing songs. I use the wind as a power source to dry my masks. I won't use a mask that's dried with a bad wind. The good winds affect your attitude, affect your spirit, your feelings. You let your mind rest and you feel the wind. . . .

My pieces start out some- where deep down inside of me. I feel that physically I just make what comes out of me spiritually. The pieces seem to mold themselves. I never really mold them.

The Indian Peoples
of the Southwest, in
Our Voices, Our Land

Find all the intuitive mediums you have tried out since beginning *Inner Voyager*. (Go back through as many entry cycles as you like.) List them below. Be sure to include *all* of them, including mediums you've explored only once or twice.

_____

_____

_____

_____

_____

_____

_____

_____

_____

Look at your list very quickly as though you'd never had experiences with the arts in question. Which stand out and call your attention? Note your impressions.

_____

_____

_____

_____

_____

_____

_____

_____

_____

_____

Suggestion: Whether or not these are arts you know well, try working with them during your psychic work in the next two cycles and then note your results in Inner Review 10.

Next, find a set of colored pens or pencils and take another look at your list of arts and mediums. Next to each one or in the space below, draw a symbol or simply make a mark in the color you most closely associate with each intuitive medium. You can also write the name of the color next to the art. Do a focusing meditation first, if you wish.

Date:

Suggestion: Compare your finished list with the Color Attributes page in Inner Resources for ideas on new possibilities each of these arts may hold for you.

Remember to update your list of Patterns and Symbols.

$$E = mc^2$$

There is nothing more difficult to take in hand, more perilous to conduct, or more uncertain in its success, than to take the lead in the introduction of a new order of things.

Niccolò Machiavelli,
The Prince

MEDITATION

DAILY EXPERIENCE

PSYCHIC WORK

And a man said, Speak to us of Self-Knowledge.

And he answered, saying:

Your hearts know in silence the secrets of the days and the nights.

But your ears thirst for the sound of your heart's knowledge.

You would know in words that which you have always known in thought.

You would touch with your fingers the naked body of your dreams.

And it is well you should.

The hidden well-spring of your soul must needs rise and run murmuring to the sea;

And the treasure of your infinite depths would be revealed to your eyes.

But let there be no scales to weigh your unknown treasure;

And seek not the depths of your knowledge with staff or sounding line.

For self is a sea boundless and measureless.

Say not, "I have found the truth," but rather, "I have found a truth."

Say not, "I have found the path of the soul." Say rather, "I have met the soul walking upon my path."

For the soul walks upon all paths.

The soul walks not upon a line, neither does it grow like a reed.

The soul unfolds itself, like a lotus of countless petals.

Kahlil Gibran, The Prophet

The Rainbow comes and
goes,
And lovely is the Rose.

William Wordsworth,
"Ode: Intimations of
Immortality"

Now that you've become familiar with some of your personal intuitive symbols (and, hopefully, also with some symbols we all have in common), you've probably started to notice how these symbols come up in all parts of your life. Try reviewing favorite books, songs, paintings, and movies to see what important symbols they contain. Consider the past as well as the present. What do the symbols that you attracted at certain times in your life (or that were attracted to you) say about qualities you were developing then or questions you wanted answered? Were you attracted to rainbows, perhaps, just as you began to seriously consider the possibility of alternate realities? Or maybe you bought a yellow bedspread to stimulate intellectual energy when working on a challenging project or studying for an important exam. How have these symbols been incorporated in your current life? How have they changed or remained the same?

MEDITATION

DAILY EXPERIENCE

PSYCHIC WORK

Singing is an easy, effective method for grounding and centering and for receiving guidance from your higher awareness.

If you think back over your favorite songs over the years, you'll probably find a few that make you feel especially calm and safe, and others that make you feel focused, energized, or strong. These are your best tuning songs. They tend to be songs that are sung in groups, since songs that evoke this reaction in one person are likely to evoke it in many. And since they make people feel good, people like to sing them when they want to feel good together. For instance, do "Amazing Grace," "Zippity Doo Dah," "Dona Nobis Pacem," " 'Tis the Gift to Be Simple," or even "I've Been Working on the Railroad" make you feel a certain way? Or do you have a favorite English madrigal or piece of choral music? Maybe for you there's a particular Beatles song.

Try your favorite songs and note how they make you feel. Does one calm you down? Does another lift you up? The former is then probably a good grounding song for you, while the latter might be good to try when you're tuning in for higher guidance during meditation. Sing or listen to your favorite songs, and see if they seem to affect any particular energy centers (see Inner Resources). If you like, make a list of your personal tuning songs. Write the words out. Experience how they make you feel.

We live in an ocean of frequencies as a fish lives in the water. The fish is unaware of the many possibilities of the medium in which he moves. So Man has been totally unaware of the possibilities of the vast ocean of frequencies in which he lives. . . . We have already discovered in the cutting of crystals how to get certain sound effects at different frequencies. This would also give us different frequencies of energies for use. . . . Remember, the universe was created by sound. Very shortly the scientists will be saying this.

V. Neal and S. Karagulla,
Through the Curtain

And God said, "Let there be light"; and there was light.
Genesis 1.3

In the beginning was the
Word, and the Word was
with God, and the Word was
God. He was in the begin-
ning with God; all things
were made through him, and
without him was not anything
made that was made. In him
was life, and the life was the
light of men. The light shines
in the darkness, and the
darkness has not overcome it.

John 1.1-5

Why indeed must "God" be a
noun? Why not a verb—the
most active and dynamic
of all?

Mary Daly,
Beyond God the Father

Who rise from flesh to spirit
know the fall:
The word outleaps the world,
and light is all.

Theodore Roethke,
"The Vigil"

The one fact that began to illuminate the area of life purpose for me personally was in the area of dermatoglyphics and fetal development. In the eighth week of pregnancy, eleven pads called Bolar pads appear on the hands of the developing fetus—one on each finger, one on each thumb, and six on each palm. As the fetus develops, these pads eventually shrink and disappear, leaving skin corrugations in their wake. By the sixteenth week those skin corrugations become permanent, and eventually become your fingerprints.

And here is the remarkable fact. When the fingerprints form as the finger pads shrink, what the prints are actually doing is forming topographical maps of the pads—a unique, permanent prenatal map of the size and shape of those pads that shows all the different ingredients that make up the recipe that is you. And here is another remarkable fact. The same type of patterned minutiae that make up our fingerprints appear as well in only a very few select patterns in the world—on sand dunes, in the wave patterns the surf leaves behind, in zebra stripes, and in certain chemical suspensions.

Some sort of high-frequency wave energy form physically imprints itself in these very few, select areas. I like to think that that high-frequency wave energy is the soul energy leaving behind its unalterable imprint in the body, an imprint which will remind us of which classes in the Earth University we have passed and which ones we have failed in past lives. It also reminds us of what we've come here to feel fulfilled in, and which hurdles we have placed in our own paths to work on remedial lessons.

What you do with this information is certainly up to you. But the unalterable blueprint of all the qualities that make you is literally "at your fingertips."

Richard Unger,
palmist and Director of the
Institute of Hand Analysis

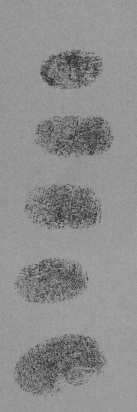

Developing awareness has a spiral, upward movement that allows you to see both where you've been and where you are at the moment, and to perceive the inherent connection between the two. Sometimes, the integration process can be a slightly bewildering one. There may be moments when you actually sense the light at the end of the tunnel and at the same time still feel kept in the dark.

Just remember in those situations there is indeed an answer—but for whatever reason you're not quite ready to see it yet. . . . This is very much like the experience we've all had as children when our mothers told us, "You'll understand when you're older." Of course, when we matured, we were able to see more clearly—and in fact could understand more from the vantage point of our broadened knowledges and experience.

Patricia Einstein,
Uncommon Sense

The explosion that is taking place because the female energy has concentrated itself and reached critical mass simply means that the formless, concealed from our view, is suddenly surfacing. It takes on a living form, emptying from a whirlpool of darkness and unconsciousness. It manifests in this world, urging us to take notice of its inherent energy, prompting us, regardless of our gender, to contact it, accept it, and creatively use it. One of the things that will most heal the separation between the male and the female is an inherent recognition that these energies are contingent upon each other and that all form contains them both. Women have masculine energy within them, as men have feminine energy. Our consciousness can guide the balancing of those two energies . . . and change the way we live in this world.

We are at that point in life where the feminine manifests itself consciously and actively in the external world, where women also use yang power. Simultaneously, men discover something new in themselves underneath their strong shells. They discover the life force, sometimes called "shakti," which is the feminine creative kundalini power.

*We all can become mani-
festors in our lives using the
intuitive guidance of the
female within, whether we are
men or women, to guide us
into conscious synergy. We
have only to embark upon the
powerful adventure of attun-
ing our awareness to the
different energies in play
around us and consciously
directing those energies for the
purpose of harmonic mani-
festation. It's a skill we were
born to learn.*

Chris Griscom,
Time Is an Illusion

MEDITATION

DAILY EXPERIENCE

PSYCHIC WORK

Consider the qualities in yourself that well up from the yin or anima energy if you are a man, or the yang or animus energy if you are a woman. It may help to first focus on this energy in your being by intuitively seeing it (is it a green cloud? a well of thick purple liquid bubbling up?), hearing it (a flute? a harp? a voice? a horn?), feeling it (fine and strong like silk? a warm, ever-present touch on your spine?), or simply knowing it (an integral part of the white energy whizzing around in your personal energy field?). Experience the energy and blend your awareness with it. When you're ready, let its individual, discrete qualities show themselves to you in the intuitive language you have chosen (pictures, sounds, feelings, knowledge). Note these qualities in *Inner Voyager*. And know that you can access this energy in yourself for its guidance whenever you like.

*Every mother and every be-
loved is forced to become the
carrier and embodiment of
this omnipresent and ageless
image, which corresponds to
the deepest reality in a man.
It belongs to him, this perilous image of Woman; she
stands for the loyalty which in
the interests of life he must
sometimes forgo; she is the
much needed compensation
for the risks, struggles, sacri-
fices that all end in disap-
pointment; she is the solace
for all the bitterness of life.
And, at the same time, she is
the great illusionist, the se-
ductress, who draws him into
life with her Maya—and not
only into life's reasonable and
useful aspects, but into its
frightful paradoxes and ambivalences where good and
evil, success and ruin, hope
and despair, counterbalance
one another. Because she is
his greatest danger she demands from a man his greatest, and if he has it in him
she will receive it. This image
is "My Lady Soul," as
Spitteler called her. I have
suggested instead the term
"anima". . . .*

C. G. Jung, Aion

Every sickness is an attempt at healing and every healing an attempt to escape from the everyday neurosis of ordinary consciousness so as to arrive at a more subtle . . . form of perception.

We see life as a relatively uniform and continuous process marked by merely peripheral changes, whereas so-called primitive cultures tend to see personal development as a series of leaps from one mode of existence to another. This is clearly shown by the traditional rites of passage conducted not only at birth, puberty, and death but especially at the breakthrough from everyday existence to a spiritual dimension. . . .

The important stages in a person's life are connected by periods of inner purification so that the individual, being properly prepared and in a clear state of mind . . . may progress to a new unburdened existence. This purification may take many forms: either purely physical . . . or intense psychic isolation . . . and actual sickness which brings internal obstacles and defilements to the surface and, indeed, expels them, thereby producing a heightened sensitivity for the process of being.

Holger Kalweit,
Dreamtime & Inner Space

Unfortunately, most of us must suffer before we can be transformed. My wife, Bobbie, and I were sitting in the kitchen when the garbage disposal jammed. I said, "What shall I do?" She said, "Just push the reset button." So I went to God and asked, "If you're such a great creator, why didn't you give us a reset button?" God answered, "I did give you a reset button, Bernie. It's called pain and suffering." It is only through pain that we change. It can be difficult to see our loved ones hurting but not changing. Our job is to love them. It is their pain that changes them, not our sermon.

Bernie S. Siegel, M.D., Love, Medicine & Miracles

Below, list Inner Review questions that are particularly important to you and your intuitive and spiritual development. Perhaps you would like to repeat or try variations on earlier Inner Review questions that seem particularly appropriate for you at this time. Or perhaps there are some creative reflections and connections you would like to make based on material from books, lectures, or workshops, or simply on issues that have come up for you in the course of using *Inner Voyager*. Feel free also to write yourself questions that may emerge in the future, but which you aren't prepared to answer right now.

_____

_____

_____

_____

_____

_____

_____

Look at Crystals, Numbers and Symbols, and Color Attributes in Inner Resources. Which individual entries in these sections seem feminine to you? Which seem masculine? And which seem neutral in regard to gender energy? (There is no "right" answer.) Note your impressions. You might try reinterpreting dream or psychic work experiences and your personal patterns and symbols in light of this new perspective.

_____

_____

_____

_____

_____

_____

_____

_____

Now answer one or more of those questions. Choose the one (or ones) that seem most useful to you at this time.

_____

_____

_____

_____

_____

_____

_____

_____

_____

_____

_____

_____

_____

_____

_____

_____

Date:

Suggestion: From now on, take time to add a personal review question to the end of every Inner Review. Or, if you'd like, go back and apply a personal review question to previous _Inner Voyager_ cycles.

We came to a small cave and sat down. I was out of breath and dripping with perspiration. . . . Zoila . . . looked calm, perhaps a little bored. Sitting there, I realized how stiff I was and how many aches and pains I had. I gazed at the fantastic view across the canyon. The sky was golden. I could see the narrow path spiral upward, and I was amazed that I had managed it. Nearby, a glint of sunlight caught my eye. I stood up, and there on a ledge was a gold Mayan mask inlaid with turquoise, emerald, and jade. The stones were carved in exquisite snake and jaguar designs. . . .

Zoila's voice had a matter-of-fact quality. "It is a beautiful trinket. You take it. It is a gift from the spirits of la caldera."

I climbed up the almost perpendicular ledge and ran my hands over the gleaming surface of the mask, brushing away the dust.

"It's worth a fortune."

"Take it."

"But I can't just take it, Zoila. Maybe it's here for a reason." . . .

I took a final look at the gorgeous mask shimmering in the sun. The bright stones glimmered alluringly. I turned away and crawled down from the ledge. The discovery had somehow made me melancholy. . . .

"When the spirits of la caldera offered you a treasure, you could not avail yourself of it."

"Why couldn't I, Zoila?"

"Because you didn't feel worthy of such riches. And what happened next? You slipped and hurt your back. Do you know why?"

"No."

"Because you're afraid to take your power. . . . You lost faith in your own capacity. . . . You are lucky you have experienced these ordeals, these lessons, for new wisdom is afoot. Be proud of yourself and what you've accomplished. Cease your struggling now."

Lynn V. Andrews,
Jaguar Woman

He who longs to strengthen
his spirit
must go beyond obedience
and respect.
He will continue to honor
some laws
but he will mostly violate
both law and custom.

Constantine Cavafy,
"Strengthening the Spirit"

The calling of Korean shamanesses expresses itself in various physiological disturbances, conscious forms of social behavior, outrageous activities, impoliteness, and a lifestyle that inverts traditional cultural values. For instance, the prospective shamaness may wear winter clothes in summer, bathe in cold water in winter, reveal secrets which are taboo to mention, or begin to tell the fortune of anyone who happens to be passing in the street.

Youngsook Kim Harvey,
Six Korean Women:
The Socialisation of
Shamans

Food for thought: Which embarrassing intuitive experience in your life actually ended up contributing greatly to your spiritual development?

There is a third stage of religious experience which . . . I will call cosmic religious feeling. It is very difficult to explain this feeling to anyone who is entirely without it, especially as there is no anthropomorphic conception of God corresponding to it.

The individual feels the nothingness of human desires and aims and the sublimity and marvellous order which reveal themselves both in Nature and in the world of thought. He looks upon individual existence as a sort of prison and wants to experience the universe as a single significant whole.

Albert Einstein,
The World as I See It

The state of Nirvana cannot be described, but it can be hinted at or suggested metaphorically. The word literally means "blowing out," as of a lamp. In Nirvana all idea of an individual personality or ego ceases to exist and there is nothing to be reborn—as far as the individual is concerned Nirvana is annihilation. But it was . . . conceived of as a transcendent state, beyond the possibility of full comprehension by the ordinary being enmeshed in the illusion of selfhood.

William Theodore de Bary, The Buddhist Tradition

"Why do I choose channeling in this life, on the conscious day-to-day level? Why am I continuing to choose it? There's two parts to that answer. One is that it helps me to grow; it helps me to integrate my personality with my environment all the better. Helps me to make more success of all the levels of my life—mental, physical, emotional, etc. Helps me to clear myself with my desires and goals. Secondly, it gives me a balance in my life—mediumship gives me balance, because it helps me stay in touch with the spiritual."

S., trance medium, in The Channeling Process, by Margo Chandley, Ph.D.

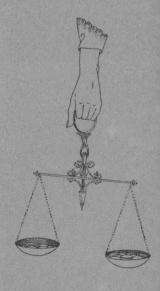

Many people say, "Okay, so you can open yourself to this great power, and this other psychic stuff comes in to you. So you're attuned." But it's not that at all. If that were the whole story, then everything would be over, your life would become passive. And I don't think life is passive; it's an active partnership with your own power source. This is the lesson my years of work have taught me. . . .

In other words, I am not just a channel. No one is just a channel; the power manifests through you from one dimension and you influence it; you are the cause that changes its direction, flow, and impact.

Sheila Petersen-Lowary,
The Fifth Dimension

DAILY EXPERIENCE

PSYCHIC WORK

May 19

I am floating in a dark space. I can still feel the effects of great acceleration. Suddenly I find myself floating above a land that is unfamiliar to me, a sci-fi landscape. I am encased in a bubble; it seems to protect me from the outside. A sadness comes over me. I know something about this land but am unable to fully remember. Then, as suddenly as I arrived, I leave and slowly approach a tremendous beam of light. My bubble is gone; I think my body is gone. My perception is somehow entirely emotional, but still, even without eyes, there is a visual image. I feel a tremendous strength in the presence of this beam of light. It is bright blue-white with a visible current to it, motion. I am overwhelmed by the feeling of having come home. This is a revelation, the discovery of something I have always known.

David Skolkin,
from a personal journal

Take a look at this beautiful illustration and write in your own, favorite inspiring quote here. What special intuitive talent in you does it speak to or reveal? What spiritual direction in your future does it augur?

There were many magical moments during the first five years of my life. These experiences with the other forms of life, other beings, and some moments when rocks spoke to me all seemed to be a normal part of life. . . . When I turned nine we moved to the countryside on the outskirts of Los Angeles. There was a walnut grove nearby that became a very important spot for me. Between the trees swept a sea of wild mustard, with very bright yellow flowers. . . . For several years I remained shorter than the mustard blanket and could stand surrounded by the fields without being visible.

A large part of my childhood was spent within these mustard fields, creating my own world, crawling around, eating their roots, digging holes and hiding myself in them. Yellow stimulates the nervous system, and my sensory perception was wonderfully enhanced in this magical world. I experienced all manner of life forms directly and personally about this time. . . .

In seventh grade . . . the introduction of algebra struck some deep chord of recognition within me. Just the sight of algebraic equations would sometimes cause my heart to bound with excitement. . . . On our first quiz, I delightedly handed in my paper within just a few minutes of the starting time. The teacher was shocked and immediately suspicious. . . . Of course I could only say that [the answers] just popped up in my mind's eye as I looked at the equations. The teacher concluded that I was cheating.

Chris Griscom,
Time Is an Illusion

When I was five or six, I'd get very scared when I went to bed at night. I used to feel a different consciousness watching me around the room—the room seemed very peopled, not good or bad, but the fact that I didn't know them but they knew me made me quite uneasy. One night I was staring out the open, lit doorway when something astonishing happened. A life-size, animated-cartoon Indian brave in headdress, beads, and loincloth suddenly peeked out at me from the side of the door frame and then disappeared. When a creative writing teacher playfully recounted a similar experience half in jest, mine suddenly swam up to the surface. His, which had something to do with a giant screen, he described as one of the great mysteries of his life, and for a long time I described mine the same way. Now, however, the mystery is at least partially solved.

Marsha David

Many recall childhood experiences that seemed mysterious at the time but, in retrospect, are clearly understood as early adventures with natural intuitive talent. Some of these remembered experiences are silly and mysterious at the same time. For instance, maybe your favorite cartoon character came to life in your bedroom to say goodnight when you were very young. Or perhaps the woods or fields "spoke" to you, or you used to play with fairies or elves.

Some of these early experiences felt wonderful. Others seemed scary or embarrassing at the time. As a group, they tend to be more "far out" and uninhibited than our first intuitive steps as adults. One very bright friend of mine routinely left his body and scooted around the classroom ceiling when he got bored with the lesson. Recalling these experiences will help you understand what was really at work at the time and will also provide you with promising new paths for intuitive exploration. Take a moment to note down any conscious memories you may have of these mysterious and wondrous childhood happenings.

Try the following meditation (after your basic centering meditation) to rediscover key childhood experiences you may have forgotten:

In your mind's eye, see yourself in the driver's seat of your favorite form of transportation (your car, a white horse, that yellow ten-speed bicycle, a river raft like Huck Finn's, or even an airplane). Begin to move. Watch the road unfold in front of you (or the earth below, or the river, or the path).

Say your present age out loud. What do you see? What is there? *Very slowly* (maybe one year a minute), count backward from your age and keep moving down the road. What places in your life show up? People from your past? What do you hear? What do your feelings tell you about what turns you should take on this path to find lost intuitive experiences? Know your vehicle will stop whenever there is an important intuitive experience to explore by the side of your route. Take as long as you need to explore each. Then get back in your waiting vehicle and continue. Speed or slow your count according to what feels natural to you.

When you reach the age of fourteen, notice a wonderful golden glow haloing your path. It's a light that protects and energizes and gives you clear insight. Feel that light around you as you move toward and through it. Keep counting. Feel yourself travel deeper and deeper into your intuitive past. Feel the protection of your family, your higher self. Seek out your early teachers, whether they be friends and family, guides, trees, or rocks. See their faces. Hear their voices. Stop to touch things, and to fully explore key experiences along the way. Know you will remember what you need to later.

When you reach infancy, see your road lead into a wonderful, soft, red, cushiony light that is the womb. Leave your transportation outside and rest inside, if you like. Know your transportation will be there waiting for you when you come out. What, if any, intuitive impressions flow over you?

When you're ready, come out of the red light and get back in the driver's seat. Now, counting upward from zero to your present age three times as quickly as before, cruise, trot, or sail back to the present, waving a fond farewell to your intuitive milestones as you go.

Note your key experiences in *Inner Voyager.* Stand up and stretch. Move around a little. Turn on the stereo. Call a friend.

—How is the koan coming?
—There is no koan.
—How is that?
—There is no koan, and which one is unimportant.
—Explain yourself, said the roshi seriously.
—The meaning of the koan is not in the koan.
—Good, said the roshi. Push forward. You are now getting somewhere.

Donald Richie, Zen Inklings

Experiment with writing without your usual rituals. If you like to use music, try writing in *Inner Voyager* in silence. Substitute your usual focusing meditation with an affirmation, or with nothing at all. If you are using the guided exercises in *Inner Voyager*, discover how you can write just as effectively without these suggestions. If you write using your own system, try *Inner Voyager*'s. If you are habitually slow and deliberate, sit down and put pen to paper without any preliminary reflection at all. If you are a naturally fast writer, sit and deliberate on your subject for at least ten minutes before writing about it. Keep up the variation for a week. Then alternate or try more new methods.

Find the intuitive experience in your previous daily entries that was most satisfying and complete for you. Note it here.

_____

_____

_____

_____

_____

_____

Take a minute to pinpoint exactly what it was about the experience that was so satisfying to you.

_____

_____

_____

_____

_____

What events, feelings, impressions, images, hunches, or other circumstances (such as atmosphere or others present) led up to this experience? What conscious intuitive preparation had you made (psychic work, meditation, workshop, long walk in the park)? Review your most recent entries or go farther back, as necessary, to answer this.

_____

_____

_____

_____

_____

What can you do to recreate these circumstances to help foster other peak intuitive experiences?

_____

_____

_____

_____

_____

_____

_____

_____

Review your list of personal review questions in Inner Review 9. Choose the one most pertinent for you today and answer it here.

_____

_____

_____

_____

_____

_____

_____

_____

_____

_____

Date: _____

Remember to update Patterns and Symbols in Inner Resources, keeping on the lookout for those that may be changing in meaning, or earlier patterns and symbols whose meaning you may be able to refine at this point.

"Construct in your imag-
ination a luminous cape, a
white cape with a hood
that is long and flowing.
You are a worker in the
light; you may as well
wear a cape that is made
of light. . . .

"With your white cape
flowing, hold your arms
up and out from your
body and turn your palms
upward. Release a mes-
sage of light or love to all
the people on this planet.
See them beginning to
awaken and to create
their own capes of lumi-
nous light as they stand
resplendent in vitality
and joy."

LaUna Huffines,
Bridge of Light

I sit at least once a day with my arms stretched out to the side and say, "I am open and receptive to all the good and abundance in the Universe." It gives me a feeling of expansion.

Louise L. Hay,
You Can Heal Your Life

MEDITATION

DAILY EXPERIENCE

PSYCHIC WORK

You can use the power of visualization and affirmation to create light and goodwill for the planet, along with your more personal goals. Triangles is a worldwide service group whose members perform the same simple meditation each day. The meditation creates and strengthens a network of light and goodwill growing throughout the world. This network establishes understanding and good relations among all people, raises the level of human consciousness and spirituality, strengthens and supports the goodwill service workers of the world, and inspires practical and constructive action on behalf of humanity.

You become a part of the Triangles network by following this simple meditation daily and by repeating the Invocation you will find when you turn the page.

First, form a triangle group consisting of yourself and two others. The members of each triangle do not have to be in the same town or even in the same country, and they do not have to meditate at the same time. Once a triangle is activated, any of its members can strengthen it.

Choose a time to sit quietly and do the triangle meditation. First, link mentally with the other members of your triangle. Next, invoke the energies of light and goodwill, and visualize these energies circulating through the apexes of your triangle, then streaming from that individual triangle through all the other triangles that have been created across the planet. Finally, repeat the Invocation to bring the same light and love downward into humanity.

The Triangles network covers ninety-two countries all over the globe, and the Triangle meditation and instructions have been translated into more than ten languages. The Reading List in Inner Resources will tell you where to get more information and materials if you would like them.

MEDITATION

DAILY EXPERIENCE

PSYCHIC WORK

The Great Invocation

From the point of Light
    within the Mind of God
Let light stream forth into the
    minds of men.
Let Light descend on earth.

From the point of Love within
    the Heart of God
Let Love stream forth into the
    hearts of men.
May Christ* return to Earth.

From the center where the
    Will of God is known
Let purpose guide the wills of
    men
The purpose which the Mas-
    ters know and serve.

From the center which we call
    the race of men.
Let the Plan of Love and
    Light work out.
And may it seal the door
    where evil dwells.

Let Light and Love and
    Power restore the Plan
    on Earth.

The Lucis Trust (Trust the
Light), which supports Triangles, a worldwide service
activity for men and women
of goodwill who believe in the
power of thought.

*Or the Messiah, the Iman
Mahdi, Lord Krishna, Lord
Maitreya, the Great Mother, the
Source, the God Within, the
Magic Presence.

DAILY EXPERIENCE

While with an eye made quiet
by the power
Of harmony, and the deep
power of joy,
We see into the life of things.

William Wordsworth,
"Lines Composed a Few
Miles Above Tintern Abbey"

MEDITATION

DAILY EXPERIENCE

PSYCHIC WORK

"To enable one to see the fairies—a pint of sallet oyle and put it into a vial glasse; and first wash it with rose-water and marygolde water; the flowers to be gathered towards the east. Wash it till the oyle becomes white, then put it into the glasse, and then put thereto the budds of hollyhocke, the flowers of marygolde, the flowers or toppes of wild thyme the budds of young hazle, and the thyme must be gathered near the side of a hill where fairies use to be; and take the grasse of a fairy throne; then all these put into the oyle in the glasse and sette it to dissolve three dayes in the sunne and then keep it for thy use."

Receipt dated 1600, from *A Garden of Herbs*, by Eleanour Sinclair Rohde

*I will come to you in the
    shape of a nightingale,
Many branches are on a tree,
    on each branch I will
    Be,
The nightingale is here, there,
    everywhere,
When you will hear it, you
    will know that I am
    here,
The nightingale who at all
    times is everywhere.*

Sufi song, in
Daughter of Fire,
by Irina Tweedie

*Once out of nature I shall
    never take
My bodily form from any
    natural thing,
But such a form as Grecian
    goldsmiths make
Of hammered gold and gold
    enamelling
To keep a drowsy Emperor
    awake;
Or set upon a golden bough
    to sing
To lords and ladies of Byzan-
    tium
Of what is past, or passing,
    or to come.*

W. B. Yeats,
"Sailing to Byzantium"

If you're in the market for some extra food for thought today, consider what there is about the bird image that makes it such a powerful channel for intuitive work. Perhaps there is at least one member of the ornithological family in your collection of personal symbols—they tend to crop up fairly often. Or maybe one particular sort of bird has resonated for you during the course of your inner reading voyages. Is it a bird's agility? The way one can perch undisturbed and unnoticed in a tree, garden, or room? The way wings have of sensing out the powerful currents of air, then using them to coast to places we only dream of?

In your next meditation, pretend you are a bird perched hidden in the branches of your most profuse problem. What do you see and hear as you look down? How does it feel? When you know all you need, simply rise up out of the problem and wing back down into yourself with your newfound insights.

Some of the most satisfying novels are those that cover several generations in a family, showing the inevitable similarities and differences between people who share a heritage, a milieu, and a whole inheritance of different-but-similar experiences. As you read, you can watch the progression as characters with different combinations of a single pool of qualities test them out in different situations with different goals. Think of novels by Charles Dickens, or by Gabriel García Márquez, or your own favorites.

You can use a simple version of this time-honored technique to gain insight about past-life experience. It's called "Life Pairings." Write down a past-life experience you've recalled as if it were a story happening to someone else. Fill in details about the place and time in which it takes place, the smell, the light, the food, the sounds, and even the more minor characters in the story, if you can. What did it really feel like to be you there and then? If you'd like, use basic focusing to get new information. You can choose an experience in which you were the only familiar character, or one involving someone who is again part of your life.

Now focus again, using your favorite meditation technique, and discover a "story incident" in your present life that resonates with the incident from your soul's past. Write this story out as if you had the same distance and empathy as you do toward the story from your past life.

When you're ready (or next time you open *Inner Voyager*), compare the two to see what additional insights you have. What's the same? What's different? And what third story could you write in a future life (or even in the future of this life) that would resolve the situation, bring it to a sense of harmonious completion, or develop the relationship to include a new area of soul growth? Visualize or affirm the resolution or development taking place, and release that newly created intention out into the Universe.

In truth there is no right or wrong. There is no polarity for all will be, as you would say, reconciled at some point in your dance through the mind/body/spirit complex which you amuse yourself by distorting in various ways at this time. This distortion is not in any case necessary. It is chosen by each of you as an alternative to understanding the complete unity of thought which binds all things. You are not speaking of similar or somewhat like entities or things. You are every thing, every being, every emotion, every event, every situation. You are unity. You are infinity. You are love/light, light/love. You are. This is the Law of One.

Ra, in The Ra Material, by Don Elkins, Carla Rueckert, and James Allen McCarty

Above, the yin-yang of a basic metaphysical issue. What are your thoughts on the ongoing conversation between unity and uniqueness? Universal authority and the authority of the individual? Surrender and self-protection? Trust and discernment? The Many and the One? How does the dance culminate in your life?

Minsky . . . sermonized, ". . . The main concern of a religion is to stop thinking, to suppress doubt." . . .
    I said, "Science feels and acts like a kind of religion a lot of the time." Minsky had heard that one before: "Everything is similar if you're willing to look that far out of focus. I'd watch that. Then you'll find that black is white. Look for differences! You're looking for similarities again. That way lies mind rot."

Stewart Brand,
The Media Lab

The Definition of Grace

I have described a whole variety of phenomena that have the following characteristics in common:

a) They serve to nurture—support, protect and enhance—human life and spiritual growth.

b) The mechanism of their action is either incompletely understandable (as in the case of physical resistance and dreams) or totally obscure (as in the case of paranormal phenomena) according to the principles of natural law as interpreted by current scientific thinking.

c) Their occurrence is frequent, routine, commonplace and essentially universal among humanity.

d) Although potentially influenced by human consciousness, their origin is outside of the conscious will and beyond the process of conscious decision-making.

Although generally regarded as separate, I have come to believe that their commonality indicates that these phenomena are part of or manifestations of a single phenomenon: a powerful force originating outside of human consciousness which nurtures the spiritual growth of human beings. For hundreds and even thousands of years before the scientific conceptualization of such things as immune globulins, dream states, and the unconscious, this force has been consistently recognized by the religious, who have applied to it the name of grace. And have sung its praise. "Amazing grace, how sweet the sound . . ."

M. Scott Peck, M.D.,
The Road Less Traveled

MEDITATION

DAILY EXPERIENCE

PSYCHIC WORK

Amazing grace! How sweet
        the sound
That saved a wretch like me!
I once was lost, but now am
        found,
Was blind, but now I see.

'Twas grace that taught my
        heart to fear,
And grace my fears relieved;
How precious did that grace
        appear
The hour I first believed!

Through many dangers, toils
        and snares,
I have already come;
'Tis grace hath brought me
        safe thus far,
And grace will lead me home.

And when we've been there
        ten thousand years,
Bright shining as the sun,
We'll have no less days to sing
        God's praise
Then when we first begun.

John Newton,
"Amazing Grace"

Consider an instance in which your intuition has provided you with information or guidance that has helped another person. In this area, is there a particular kind of information that you intuit more often than others? Or are there particular areas in which you seem to have greater accuracy when helping others? Are there particular circumstances in which you are likely to receive a request for information? Review cycle 11 or go as far back in *Inner Voyager* as you like.

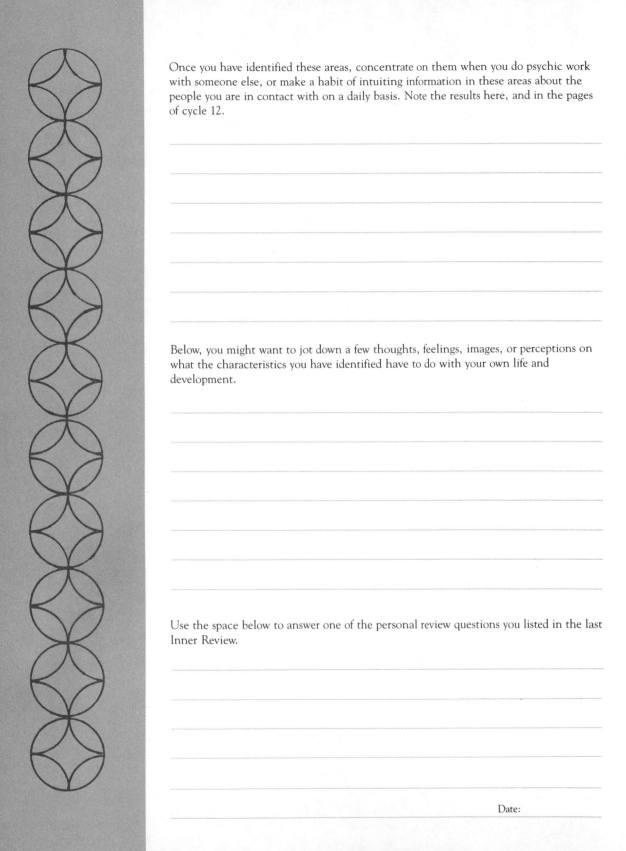

Once you have identified these areas, concentrate on them when you do psychic work with someone else, or make a habit of intuiting information in these areas about the people you are in contact with on a daily basis. Note the results here, and in the pages of cycle 12.

_____

_____

_____

_____

_____

_____

Below, you might want to jot down a few thoughts, feelings, images, or perceptions on what the characteristics you have identified have to do with your own life and development.

_____

_____

_____

_____

_____

_____

_____

Use the space below to answer one of the personal review questions you listed in the last Inner Review.

_____

_____

_____

_____

Date: _____

The evolution of consciousness, of thought, of enlightenment, is a powerful experience. Have fun with it.

Theo, in
The Fifth Dimension,
by Sheila Petersen-Lowary

Each life is charmed . . . and you must never forget it. . . . You are magic. You charm the air so that it thickens into your body wherever you are. . . . But you have to remember that your life is charmed. . . . But people are also very creative . . . magic again! . . . so they make up gods of this and that, and realms and spheres, and maps to chart out in advance where magic might be taking them so they don't get surprised, which is silly because magic goes where it wants to, which is everywhere. And when you try to map it out in advance, you really cut yourself short. . . . If you forget what magic is, then you're liable to think that your map is the only real one, and all others are false. You get in a terrible bind, fighting over which way is right, which road or map, while all the time magic is what makes the maps.

Systems of magic are silly, too, and all of them are really based upon doubt. Magic is considered so tenuous that someone has to be at it all the time, making spells or paying someone else to do it. And the spells all have to be done just right, so people concentrate on how to do this spell or another. This gets very complicated. . . . But everything is a spell. Your words and thoughts are spells.

Jane Roberts,
The Further Education
of Oversoul Seven

The body is a tool, a vehicle that you have created to focus on certain points within the self that you wish to transform in a most efficient way. All of the systems in your body are built precisely for that transformation. You will see that in your work, in the nervous system, in the automatic functioning of the body, down to the very cells of the bones. You will find each portion of the body a delicate and beautiful tool for the use of transformation. It is not a burden. It is a gift. It is unfortunate that most human beings do not understand that.

The greater portion of you that is not completely incarnated . . . decides whether or not the best place for you for the next transformative work is in a body or not. And when you have made full use of these physical vehicles . . . you end . . . the wheel of incarnations. . . . It simply is that you no longer need this tool [of a physical body] to separate out a linear time, and a three dimensional space that makes it easier for you to see the particular points [of your greater self] that you wish to transform.

Enlightenment goes on in another way. We are also clearing ourselves and moving toward God. There are an infinite number of stages. . . . At this point you can only go to a certain height because your perception ability is not that broad. . . . As the darkness fades, the transformation process becomes one of creativity rather than of healing.

Heyoan, in Hands of Light, by Barbara Ann Brennan

Hogan of turquoise flint,
The One of turquoise flint
    that will be built up.
Born-for-Water . . .
arise to protect me. . . .
The One of turquoise color
    who cannot be shot by
    an arrow,
That which cannot be harmed
    being inside you,
With them arise to protect
    me. . . .
From your forehead a
    Tongue-eater of tur-
    quoise flint,
With it arise to protect me.
Your turquoise shields, which
    are white in the middle,
Your shield, the Big Yellow
    Snake and the Big
    White Snake,
The Ones who have come
    together, lying criss-
    crossed through the
    shield:
Your shield you will place
    before me for protection.
Sunwise you will carry it
    around me,
You will place it in front of
    me for protection.
Beyond this hold back the
    danger from me.
So then I will overcome dan-
    ger (it will be smaller
    than I am) . . .
Beyond it danger has passed
    by me.
Behind it I will survive. . . .
I have survived! I have sur-
    vived! . . .
For many more years! For
    many more years!

Navajo protection prayer,
in Navajo Mountain and
Rainbow Bridge Religion,
by Karl W. Luckert

If you like, you can use the intuitive storytelling skills you've explored to sense out the inter-life (or Bardo) experience of a loved one who has recently passed away and to understand transformations that may be taking place.

If you're grieving, keeping in touch on the soul level from a respectful distance can help you to heal and evolve, too. If your spiritual point of view includes sending love and light to those who are departed, the exercise can help you to do so in a more focused way. And in the bargain, what you uncover will surely give you another piece in the puzzle that reveals the nature of the ongoing flow of life and/or awareness.

Get comfortable, center, and focus gently on a sound, image, crystal, or affirmation.

When you're ready, gently expand your focus and search it for the image or sound that is the first key to your loved one's current experience. It is already there in your awareness. You need only to locate it and focus in on it. It is like the name of an old friend you have to look for when you run into that friend on the street after many years. Don't wrack your brains, just widen and fine-tune your focus until it comes.

Once you have that image or sound, open your eyes and describe it in *Inner Voyager*. What kind of scene does it belong in? Describe the scene.

Where is your friend or loved one? What is going on? What is being said? Keep on "writing" out the scene, and seeing it as a little fable, fairy tale, or mythological story. Whenever it seems to ebb, close your eyes, focus, and tune your awareness until a new image comes. Keep going until the story seems complete. You may even want to stop and work in "installments" over several days or even once a week for a longer time in the Psychic Work section.

The sun! The sun! And all
we can become!
And the time ripe for running
to the moon!
In the long fields, I leave my
father's eye;
And shake the secrets from
my deepest bones;
My spirit rises with the rising
wind.

Theodore Roethke,
"What Can I Tell
My Bones?"

MEDITATION

DAILY EXPERIENCE

PSYCHIC WORK

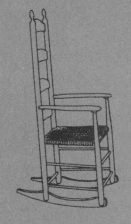

*The different kinds of vice,
the use of drugs, in the literal
or metaphorical sense of the
word, all such things con-
stitute the search for a state
where the beauty of the world
will be tangible. The mistake
lies precisely in the search for
a special state. False mysticism is another form of this
error.*

*Simone Weil,
Waiting on God*

The way is broad, reaching
    left as well as right.
The myriad creatures depend
    on it for life yet it claims
    no authority.
It accomplishes its task yet
    lays claim to no merit.
It clothes and feeds the myr-
    iad creatures yet lays
    no claim to being their
    master.
Forever free of desire, it can
    be called small; yet, as
    it lays no claim to being
    master when the myriad
    creatures turn to it, it
    can be called great.
It is because it never attempts
    itself to be great that it
    succeeds in becoming
    great.

Lao Tzu, Tao Te Ching

One night, I was practicing Therapeutic Touch and decided to hold my boyfriend's hands (not telling him what I was doing). I felt heat coming from the chakras of my hand, but it wasn't as much as I had felt in class. I attempted to send my energy across the junction of space between our hands. He did not acknowledge any sensation, but I observed an occasional twitch in his thumb, so I stopped and went over to my dog, who was lying on her belly, head up.

I tried an Assessment, but felt no difference. I then placed my hand at the back of her neck without touching her, about an inch away, and left it there. Shortly, she sighed and put her head down, apparently to get more comfortable. Soon after, she began to twitch occasionally, down to and including her tail, and then she went to sleep.

I concluded that something must have happened due to the similarity of twitches in response to my attempts to transfer energy. So I went back to my guy, who was dozing by this time, but not fully asleep, and began an Assessment from his neck to his pelvic area. I thought I felt a greater concentration of energy in the area of his stomach, just below the esophageal sphincter, so I left my hand there for a little while without touching him, waiting for a response. When I thought I felt a difference, although it *was mild, I tried to move the energy towards his feet. He responded, half unconscious, "H'm that feels good," but I wasn't touching him. The time involved was only about three minutes. As soon as I stopped, he mumbled: "Thank you. I feel so much more relaxed," and immediately fell asleep.*

M.O.S., in The Therapeutic Touch, by Dolores Krieger, Ph.D., R.N.

MEDITATION

DAILY EXPERIENCE

PSYCHIC WORK

In the early part of this century, James Joyce pioneered the technique called stream of consciousness, which has greatly influenced modern fiction. In stream of consciousness, the words on the page become the literal stream of a character's awareness and thoughts: no grammar, no sentences, no paragraphs, just a flow of experience expressed in word and sound.

Stream of consciousness has extraliterary uses, too. Use it first thing in the morning, or whenever you like, to intuitively sense the flow of energy in your environment, the moods of others around you, or even the larger state of your peer group, your community, or the world.

Do your favorite focusing and relaxing meditation. End the meditation by placing your focus at the level you would like to intuit—your immediate environment, the atmosphere created by those whom you will be dealing with during the day, and on up through the more humanitarian levels or beyond. You might want to use the Universe Blend meditation, described earlier in *Inner Voyager*, to set your focus.

Once the focus is set, start to write the words and sounds and to describe the images, feelings, and concepts your awareness receives. Imagine yourself gently pulling a cord of energy and describing it in words, even as you follow that cord farther above you, or all around you, into an endless skein. Relax and let impressions flow through your awareness and onto your paper. When you're done, take a look and see what your stream of collective consciousness tells you.

MEDITATION

DAILY EXPERIENCE

PSYCHIC WORK

What she had begun to learn was the weight of liberty. Freedom is a heavy load, a great and strange burden for the spirit to undertake. It is not easy. It is not a gift given, but a choice made, and the choice may be a hard one. The road goes upward towards the light; but the laden traveler may never reach the end of it. . . .

They came, after the sunrises and sunsets, the still days and the icy winds of their winter voyage, to the Inmost Sea. . . .

Tenar sat in the stern, erect, in her ragged cloak of black. She looked at the ring around her wrist, then at the crowded, many-colored shore and the palaces and the high towers. . . . [Ged] leapt up onto the pier and turned, holding out his hand to her. "Come!" he said smiling, and she rose, and came. Gravely she walked beside him up the white streets of Havnor, holding his hand, like a child coming home.

Ursula K. Le Guin,
The Tombs of Atuan

Always the battle of the Spiritual Warrior is with the self. Finding a will through action, yet unattached to outcomes, remaining mindful that all you can really do is stay out of your own way and let the Will of Heaven flow through you—these are among the hallmarks of the Spiritual Warrior.

Embodied in this Rune is the sword of discrimination that enables you to cut away the old, the dead, the extraneous. And yet . . . comes certain knowledge that the universe always has the first move. Patience is the virtue of this Rune, and it recalls the words of St. Augustine that "the reward of patience is patience."

Ralph Blum,
The Book of Runes

I want, by understanding myself, to understand others. I want to be all that I am capable of becoming so that I may be . . . . a child of the sun. . . . This all sounds very strenuous and serious. But now that I have wrestled with it, it's no longer so. I feel happy—deep down. All is well.

Katherine Mansfield,
last entry in her Journal

DAILY EXPERIENCE

PSYCHIC WORK

Congratulations! You have finished twelve cycles in intuitive and spiritual discovery. Pause a moment to take a deep breath. Then acknowledge your achievement with a ceremony all your own. Light a candle. Play a special song. Break bread. Or do all three or anything else that seems right to you! Describe your ceremony here.

_____

_____

_____

_____

_____

_____

_____

_____

_____

Do a focusing meditation, and review your progress over the time you spent while keeping your journal. Which five intuitive or spiritual successes stand out most vividly in your mind? List them below.

_____

_____

_____

_____

_____

_____

_____

_____

_____

_____

Now acknowledge yourself for these successes by describing them to your closest friend or peer in intuitive development. If this person also has an inner voyage, you can exchange. Make notes on this experience here.

_____

_____

_____

_____

_____

_____

_____

Search for your five greatest intuitive challenges, and list them. Share these with a friend, too.

_____

_____

_____

_____

_____

_____

_____

_____

Date: _____

Suggestion: Affirm that you will embark on a new inner voyage and that progress in these five areas, along with many surprises along the way, lit by the light of your new intuitive strengths, will be your destination.

INNER RESOURCES

The following pages provide a brief overview of many of the intuitive traditions you may be inclined to explore as you embark on your inner voyage:

Color Attributes

Astrological and Planetary Attributes

Crystal Attributes

Numbers and Their Symbols

The Major Chakras

The Seven Bodies

The Tree of Life

The Great Circles of the Earth Traditions

The Elements (Chinese and Western)

The Seven Rays

The Major Arcana of the Tarot

Myths and Archetypes

Since some of these may be familiar to you and others not, some general definitions are provided below.

But first a word about these traditions. By now you have probably discovered that intuitive systems are not inherently logical or rational. There are even occasional contradictions among psychic arts, as well as striking correspondences. Because the collective wisdom of each art has evolved through different cultures, times, and individual points of view, each expresses the Infinite via the symbols, images, and analogies most meaningful to those who created it. You will probably find that some systems seem to carry more meaning for you than others. So which of them you pursue further will be determined somewhat by your own personal reference points and inner guidance.

In the pages that follow, each intuitive system is described by key words or phrases. These are attributes that you can use to apply to specific situations in your life.

If your purpose is to interpret an intuitive experience of your own that has involved an element of one of these systems, decide which word or phrase provided in the key seems closest in meaning to your experience. For instance, if you became aware of the solar plexus chakra during meditation, you might refer to the chakra section and notice that a key word for that chakra is power. If this has come in a period when you were feeling great demands at work, you might interpret that key either as a need to assert yourself more, or perhaps as a need to fortify yourself better physically and emotionally to get through this period.

After keys are given, correspondences are provided to the other intuitive traditions most relevant to the one being described. Thus, for example, in the Astrological Attributes section you will find a correspondence to a color, precious stone, archetype, numerological equivalent, and musical note for each of the twelve signs.

When you're looking for a more detailed treatment of any one of these rich and satisfying subjects, consult the Reading List at the end of Inner Resources.

DEFINITIONS

Color Attributes: Symbolic and energetic qualities of the colors of the spectrum.

Astrological and Planetary Attributes: Qualities, energies, and influences of the twelve signs and nine planets.

Crystal Attributes: Properties of the most common stones for inner healing, balance, empowerment, and increased awareness.

Numbers and Their Symbols: The universal qualities and attributes that are embodied in the numbers 1 to 9, and the symbols that embody the qualities of each.

The Major Chakras: The major centers of the energy system that is contained within each of us, along with such other bodily systems as the respiratory, circulatory, and nervous systems. The condition of the chakras at any time is said to influence the strength and focus of our survival instinct, physical health, emotions, thoughts, and creative, intuitive, and spiritual faculties. The word *chakra* means wheel in Sanskrit.

The Seven Bodies: Esoteric tradition describes six energetic bodies or energy layers beyond the physical body. One aspect of our awareness (instinct, feeling, thought, dream, higher self, state of inner perfection, or the light body) is associated with each. They can be imagined as six layers of light, each of which has individual characteristics and extends beyond the physical body. The sight of the energetic bodies extending beyond the physical self is what we call the aura.

The Tree of Life: A mystical Jewish symbol consisting of ten spheres, or sephiroth, each of which symbolizes an essential creative quality, and the twenty-two paths that can be drawn between them. The qualities of each sephirah and the relationships between them are said to contain within them all possibilities of experience. Each of the paths is a path of spiritual growth, and each path corresponds to one of the Major Arcana cards of the Tarot.

The Great Circles of the Earth Traditions: The Sioux, Cheyenne, and followers of the religion of the Great Goddess all use circles marked with the Four Directions to center, raise power, and describe and nourish spiritual growth. Each direction is associated with a time of year, a color, an attribute, an animal, and, sometimes, a spiritual tool.

The Elements (Western and Chinese): The creative principle or essential life force expressed as interacting forces of nature, and as defined by each culture.

The Seven Rays: Described in the work of Alice Bailey, the influential metaphysical authority, the Seven Rays are the seven primary forces into which the white brilliance of the Infinite (or ultimate creative force or life principle) refracts on its way to becoming matter. Each ray has a color, an esoteric master, and an essential quality.

The Major Arcana of the Tarot: The Tarot is a deck of seventy-eight cards used to intuitively predict trends in life and to tap the archetypal energies within us that may be dominant at particular moments. No one really knows where Tarot began, although both Egypt and medieval Europe are sometimes offered as the places where it originated. The twenty-two Major Arcana cards most strongly express the archetypical or spiritual energies at work within us. Each Major Arcana card is also associated with an astrological sign or planet and a path on the Tree of Life.

Myths and Archetypes: Myths are universal stories from past and present that bring richness, depth, inner healing, understanding, and power to our lives. Archetypes are the characters (for example, King Arthur) or images (for example, The Wheel of Fortune) that express specific universal energies or principles. Myths and archetypes often act on the unconscious without requiring our conscious participation or effort, but we can also approach them to bring the specific qualities they embody into our lives. Myths and archetypes can also be understood as the creative principle or life force expressed through story and character.

This chart is designed to enable you to apply the basics of color theory to your own psychic work, meditation, and daily experiences. Although essential ideas about color attributes often remain constant through the ages and from culture to culture, specific meanings can vary. For example, in some literature of the ancient Near East, blue was God's color. In the West today, white is commonly seen as the most spiritual color (as it was by Far Eastern and Mediterranean sources in ancient times), while blue is most closely associated with tranquility, harmony, balance, and peace. Be aware, therefore, that colors can have different meanings for you.

Keep track of your personal associations and interpretations of each color as your thoughts evolve. Incorporate into your personal framework the information below that works best for you, and file the rest away for possible future reference.

To interpret secondary colors, simply blend the meanings of component colors. For example, in thinking about apricot, blend interpretations of yellow, orange, and white. Positive attributes are associated with clear, pure, or vibrant hues of the color in question, while negative attributes are most often associated with muddy, darkened, or dulled tones.

For more information on chakras and sephiroth, see the sections of Inner Resources called The Major Chakras and The Tree of Life.

BLACK

Basic attributes: Void, receptivity, absence

Positive aspects: Creative void, possibility, state of readiness, anticipation, state of grace (velvety black)

Negative aspects: Waning or absent life force, illness, being unprotected, deep forgetfulness, thwarted ambition that leads to the preceding qualities (dull black)

Chakra correspondence: None

Sephirah: Binah (Understanding)

Musical notes: None

BROWN

Basic attributes: Earthiness, sensuality

Positive aspects: Practicality, pragmatism, respect for the material world, sensual awareness

Negative aspects: Avarice, selfishness, sluggishness, sensory excess

Chakra correspondence: None

Sephirah: Malkuth (The Kingdom)

Musical notes: None or C

RED

Basic attributes: Energy, passion

Positive aspects: Vitality, drive, exuberance, sexual energy, loving nature

Negative aspects: Frenzy, aggression, anger, domination, irritability, frustration, sexual excess

Chakra correspondence: First (Base chakra)

Sephirah: Geburah (Judgment)

Musical note: C

ORANGE

Basic attributes: Courage, esteem, purification

Positive aspects: Self-esteem, pride, bravery, ambition

Negative aspects: Arrogance, egotism, insensitivity

Chakra correspondence: Second (Spleen chakra)

Sephirah: Chod (Glory)

Musical notes: C sharp/ D flat, D

YELLOW

Basic attributes: Mental functions, precision, vision

Positive aspects: Intelligence, clarity, balance, being centered, self-knowledge

Negative aspects: Excessive caution, rigidity, fear of risk, manipulation, submissiveness, low self-awareness

Chakra correspondence: Third (Solar chakra)

Sephirah: Tiphereth (Beauty)

Musical notes: D sharp/ E flat, E

GREEN

Basic attributes: Love, growth, healing, change, abundance, new substance, compassion, balance

Positive aspects: Love, growth, healing, change, abundance, new substance, compassion, balance

Negative aspects: Jealousy, "going to seed," waste, residue

Chakra correspondence: Fourth (Heart chakra)

Sephirah: Netzach
(Victory)

Musical notes: F, F sharp/
G flat

PINK

Basic attributes: Love,
beauty, harmony of
emotions

Positive aspects:
Compassion, acceptance,
tenderness, joy

Negative aspects:
Sentimentality, emotional
self-indulgence, emotional
falsity

Chakra correspondence:
Fourth (Heart chakra)

Sephirah: None

Musical notes: F, F sharp/
G flat

TURQUOISE

Basic attributes: Creativity,
expression, will, thought

Positive aspects: Self-expression, communication,
communicating alternate
realities, discipline, artistic
creation, idealism

Negative aspects: Petty tyr-
anny, self-absorption, control, imposition, reserve,
withdrawal, unrespon-
siveness

Chakra correspondence:
Fifth (Throat chakra)

Sephirah: None

Musical notes: G, G sharp/
A flat

BLUE

Basic attributes: Tranquility,
calm, integration, truth

Positive aspects: Devotion,
spiritual security, healing,
relaxation, feeling comfortable with oneself, teaching

Negative aspects:
Complacency, indolence,
lack of spiritual focus

Chakra correspondence:
Fifth or sixth (Throat or
third eye chakra)

Sephirah: Chesed (Mercy)

Musical notes: A, A sharp/
B flat

INDIGO

Basic attributes: Vision,
innovation, intuition

Positive aspects: Insight,
clarity, intuitiveness,
invention

Negative aspects:
Eccentricity, insensitivity,
disobedience, rebel-
liousness

Chakra correspondence:
Sixth (Third eye chakra)

Sephirah: None

Musical notes: A, A sharp/
B flat

VIOLET

Basic attributes:
Spirituality, ceremony,
rhythm, quest, mastery

Positive aspects: Self-
esteem, spiritual growth,
fulfillment

Negative aspects:
Overbearingness, lack of
focus, being emotionally
distant, dilettantism

Chakra correspondence:
Sixth and seventh (Third
eye and crown chakras)

Sephirah: Jesod (Foundation)

Musical note: B

MAGENTA

Basic attributes: Intuition,
inspiration

Positive aspects: Intuition,
inspiration, creative vitality

Negative aspects:
Imprudence

Chakra correspondence:
Related to first, fourth,
sixth, and seventh (Base,
heart, third eye, and crown
chakras)

Sephirah: None

Musical note: B

SILVER/GRAY

Basic attributes:
Communication, intuition

Positive aspects:
Communication of spiritual
truth, infusion of spirit in
matter, private enlightenment

Negative aspects:
Depression, fear, sadness

Chakra correspondence: A
chord of the seventh
(Crown chakra)

Sephirah: Chokmah
(Wisdom)

Musical notes: G sharp/
A flat

GOLD

Basic attributes: Life force,
spiritual vitality, spiritual
substance and strength,
spiritual service

Positive aspects: Life force,
spiritual vitality, spiritual
substance and strength,
spiritual service

Negative aspects: None

Chakra correspondence:
Third or seventh (Solar or
crown chakra)

Sephirah: None

Musical note: D (some-
times E)

WHITE

Basic attributes: Purity, integration, spirit, cleansing,
universal force and energy,
divinity, protection, peace-
fulness

Positive aspects: Purity, integration, spirit, cleansing,
universal force and energy,
divinity, protection, peace-
fulness

Negative aspects: None

Chakra correspondence:
Seventh (Crown chakra)

Sephirah: Kether (The
Crown)

Musical notes: The full oc-
tave (C to B)

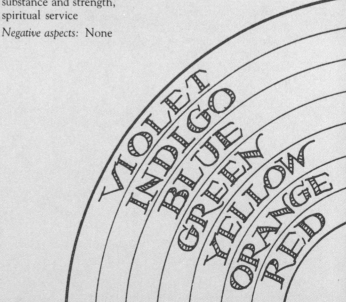

The dates for the sun signs often vary slightly from year to year, so check an ephemeris (a guide to planetary positions throughout the year) or another reputable source for the exact dates for a particular year. The information provided below on each sign includes some of the colors, mythological archetypes, and precious stones and crystals most often associated with the sign in question, in addition to other symbols and qualities. Consider this select assortment a private storehouse from which you can pick and choose according to what feels right for your needs. The archetypes refer to myths and symbols from different cultures that, when studied, provide insight about different aspects of the sign in question. See the Reading List for some good books that can aid your explorations.

ASTROLOGICAL SIGNS

ARIES

Dates: 3/20–4/19

Symbol: Ram

Element: Fire

Polarity: Positive

Quality: Cardinal

House: First

Ruling planet: Mars

Color: Bright red

Precious stones: Diamond, garnet, ruby

Key phrase: I am

Archetypes: The Quest of Hercules, Jason and the Golden Fleece, the Goddess Athena (Greek myth); The Chariot (Tarot)

Part of the body: Head

Numerological equivalent: 9

Musical note: C

TAURUS

Dates: 4/20–5/19

Symbols: Bull, crescent moon

Element: Earth

Polarity: Negative

Quality: Fixed

House: Second

Ruling planet: Venus

Color: Deep blue

Precious stones: Emerald, sapphire, rose quartz

Key phrase: I have, I build

Archetypes: Hephaestus the Forger, Aphrodite, King Minos and the Minotaur (Greek myth); The Tower (Tarot)

Parts of the body: Throat, neck

Numerological equivalent: 6

Musical note: C sharp/D flat

GEMINI

Dates: 5/20–6/19

Symbol: Twins

Element: Air

Polarity: Positive

Quality: Mutable

House: Third

Ruling planet: Mercury

Color: Blue

Precious stones: Aquamarine, turquoise, clear quartz

Key phrase: I think

Archetypes: Hermes as messenger, magician, and thief, the Dioscuri (Greek myth); Saint-Exupery's Little Prince; The Magician (Tarot)

Parts of the body: Shoulders, arms, lungs

Numerological equivalent: 5

Musical note: D

CANCER

Dates: 6/20–7/22

Symbol: Crab

Element: Water

Polarity: Negative

Quality: Cardinal

House: Fourth

Ruling planet: Moon

Color: Green

Precious stones: Pearl, moonstone, opal, aventurine

Key phrase: I care

Archetypes: Demeter, Medusa, Orpheus (Greek myth); Kali (Hindu myth);

The Empress (Tarot)

Part of the body: Stomach

Numerological equivalents: 2, 7

Musical note: D sharp/E flat

LEO

Dates: 7/23–8/22

Symbol: Lion

Element: Fire

Polarity: Positive

Quality: Fixed

House: Fifth

Ruling planet: Sun

Colors: Orange, yellow

Precious stones: Tigereye, citrine, diamond, topaz

Key phrases: I protect, I will

Archetypes: Apollo; Samson and Delilah; Aslan the Lion (C. S. Lewis' *Chronicles of Narnia*); Penelope (*The Odyssey*); Strength, The Sun (Tarot)

Parts of the body: Heart, back, solar plexus

Numerological equivalents: 1, 4

Musical note: E

VIRGO

Dates: 8/23–9/22

Symbol: The Virgin, Harvest Goddess, Sphinx

Element: Earth

Polarity: Negative

Quality: Mutable

House: Sixth

Ruling planet: Mercury

Color: Blue

Precious stones: Amazonite, agate, pink jasper

Key phrases: I analyze, I perceive, I serve

Archetypes: Hermes as healer or counselor, Aristaeus (Greek myth); Merlin the Magician (Arthurian cycle); Isis (Egyptian myth); Judgment (Tarot)

Part of the body: Intestines

Numerological equivalent: 5

Musical note: F

LIBRA

Dates: 9/23–10/22

Symbol: Scales

Element: Air

Polarity: Positive

Quality: Cardinal

House: Seventh

Ruling planet: Venus

Colors: Pale blue, pink

Precious stones: Opal, blue aventurine, pink tourmaline, kunzite

Key phrase: I harmonize

Archetypes: The Judgment of Paris, Aphrodite as partner and creative force, Odysseus (Greek myth); The Lovers (Tarot)

Part of the body: Kidneys

Numerological equivalent: 6

Musical note: F sharp/G flat

SCORPIO

Dates: 10/23–11/20

Symbols: Scorpion, curled serpent, phoenix

Element: Water

Polarity: Negative

Quality: Fixed

House: Eighth

Ruling planets: Mars, Pluto

Colors: Deep red, black

Precious stones: Topaz, bloodstone, garnet, obsidian, smoky quartz

Key phrase: I desire

Archetypes: Helen of Troy, Persephone (Greek myth); Gilgamesh (ancient Babylonian legend); the conversion of Paul (New Testament); The High Priestess, Death (Tarot)

Part of the body: Sexual organs

Numerological equivalent: 9

Musical note: G

SAGITTARIUS

Dates: 11/21–12/20

Symbols: Archer, centaur

Element: Fire

Polarity: Positive

Quality: Mutable

House: Ninth

Ruling planet: Jupiter

Colors: Indigo, violet

Precious stones: Turquoise, sodolite, lapis lazuli

Key phrases: I seek, I see

Archetypes: Hercules and Chiron the Centaur, Zeus, Bellerophon and Pegasus (Greek myth); The Hierophant (Tarot)

Part of the body: Thighs

Numerological equivalent: 3

Musical note: G sharp/A flat

CAPRICORN

Dates: 12/21–1/19

Symbol: Goat

Element: Earth

Polarity: Negative

Quality: Cardinal

House: Tenth

Ruling planet: Saturn

Colors: Black, green

Precious stones: Jet, smoky quartz, onyx, malachite, green tourmaline

Key phrase: I use

Archetypes: Kronos, Pan, King Midas (Greek myth); the Unicorn (troubador songs); The Hermit (Tarot)

Parts of the body: Knees, bones

Numerological equivalent: 8

Musical note: A

AQUARIUS

Dates: 1/20–2/19

Symbol: Water bearer

Element: Air

Polarity: Positive

Quality: Fixed

House: Eleventh

Ruling planets: Uranus, Saturn

Color: Electric blue

Precious stones: Sapphire, aquamarine, gem silica

Key phrases: I differ, I know

Archetypes: Peter Pan; Parsifal and other Grail seekers (Arthurian cycle); Atalanta (Greek myth); The Star (Tarot)

Parts of the body: Ankles, nervous system, circulatory system

Numerological equivalents: 4, 1

Musical note: A sharp/B flat

PISCES

Dates: 2/20–3/20

Symbol: Fish

Element: Water

Polarity: Negative

Quality: Mutable

House: Twelfth

Ruling planets: Neptune, Jupiter

Color: Deep purple

Precious stone: Amethyst

Key phrases: I believe, I merge

Archetypes: Telemachus and the Dolphin, Dionysus (Greek myth); Teresa of Avila (Christian saint); Temperance (Tarot)

Part of the body: Feet

Numerological equivalent: 3

Musical note: B

PLANETS

SUN

Rules sign of: Leo

Rules astrological house: Five

Governs: Vitality, individuality, creative powers, self-expression, fatherhood, natural authority and leadership, heads of state, gambling

Sephirah: Tiphereth (Beauty)

Ray: Second

Number: 1

Element: Fire

Polarity: Positive

Musical note: D

MOON

Rules sign of: Cancer

Rules astrological house: Four

Governs: Emotions, relationships to women (mothers, wives), mother-child relationship, maternal instinct, the night, the commonplace, water (the sea, travel by water, rain, tides)

Sephirah: Jesod (Foundation)

Ray: Fourth

Number: 3 or 9

Element: Water

Polarity: Negative

Musical note: G sharp/A flat

MERCURY

Rules sign of: Gemini

Rules astrological house: Three

Governs: Communication (including travel, touch, telephones, speaking, writing), intelligence and concrete mind, humor, creativity, science, memory, versatility and dexterity, thievery and tricks, signing of documents, neighbors and siblings

Sephirah: Chod (Glory)

Ray: Fourth

Number: 1 or 4

Element: Air

Polarity: Bivalent (can be positive or negative, depending on context)

Musical note: E

VENUS

Rules signs of: Taurus and Libra

Rules astrological houses: Two and seven

Governs: Love, beauty, harmony, attraction, receptive sexuality, charm and sociability, companionship, ability to form partnerships of all kinds, money and possessions, lovers and female relatives

Sephirah: Netzach (Victory)

Ray: Fifth

Number: 5, 6, or 7

Element: Earth or Air

Polarity: Negative

Musical note: F sharp/G flat

MARS

Rules sign of: Aries

Rules astrological house: One

Governs: Strength, energy, anger, active expression, desire and motivation of all kinds, aggressive sexuality, violence and rage, stamina and productivity, everything sharp, intense, and acute (such as surgical instruments, weapons, pain, sarcasm), fire, the military

Sephirah: Geburah (Judgment)

Ray: Sixth

Number: 9

Element: Fire

Polarity: Positive

Musical note: C

JUPITER

Rules sign of: Sagittarius

Rules astrological houses: Nine and twelve

Governs: Values (religions, ethical, moral), abstract mind, the search for truth, luck, prosperity, abundance, opportunity, generosity, public acclaim, obesity, publishing, foreign interests, legal affairs

Sephirah: Chesed (Mercy)

Ray: Second

Number: 3

Element: Fire

Polarity: Positive

Musical note: B flat/A sharp

SATURN

Rules sign of: Capricorn

Rules astrological houses: Ten and eleven

Governs: Contraction, solidification, discipline, obedience, responsibility, patience, persistence, structure, organization, realism, older people, authority figures, buildings and construction, history, time, knowledge, karma

Sephirah: Binah (Understanding)

Ray: Third

Number: 8

Element: Earth

Polarity: Positive

Musical note: A

URANUS

Rules sign of: Aquarius (with Saturn)

Rules astrological house: Eleven (with Saturn)

Governs: Change, innovation, disruption, humanitarianism, altruism, social reform, rebellion, originality, invention, genius, astrology and positive occultism, discoveries, earthquakes, homosexuality, electricity, the avant-garde

Sephirah: Undetermined

Ray: Seventh

Number: 4

Element: Air

Polarity: Positive

Musical note: E

NEPTUNE

Rules sign of: Pisces (with Jupiter)

Rules astrological house: Twelve (with Jupiter)

Governs: Imagination, vision, mysticism, rhythm, the unconscious, escapism

(substance abuse, delusion), illusions, mediums and seances, bisexuality, lies, camouflage, secrets and everything hidden, cloudy, or hallucinatory, salt water and oceans (with Cancer)

Sephirah: Undetermined

Ray: Sixth

Number: 7

Element: Water

Polarity: Undetermined

Musical note: G sharp/ A flat

PLUTO

Rules sign of: Scorpio (with Aries)

Rules astrological houses: Eight; One (with Aries)

Governs: Mass destiny, transformation and regeneration of all kinds, destruction, death, reincarnation, witchcraft, corruption, organized crime,

atomic power, the unleashing and recycling of energy of all kinds

Sephirah: Undetermined

Ray: First

Number: Undetermined

Element: Water

Polarity: Undetermined

Musical note: C

Jung observed that the crystal, with its magical fusion of perfect form and earthly matter, is one of the most powerful universal symbols for the self. Few people would disagree. Many people feel crystals heal, empower, and balance. Others love crystals because they are beautiful and because they serve as wonderful reminders or affirmations of qualities we are developing in our lives.

Below are the most commonly accepted attributes of the most popular crystals and gemstones. As with all interpretations, it is important that you balance these ideas with your own feelings, experience, and intuition. Use this information as a guide and also consult the colors of the chakras that correspond to the colors of the crystals or gemstones under consideration.

AMETHYST

Eases excessive mental activity (such as insomnia, worry, intellectual overstimulation); increases spiritual awareness; lifts depression; develops receptive energy and calmness in body, mind, and emotions; eases creative work; develops the receptive, spiritual aspect of the seventh chakra and soothes associated physical conditions.

AQUAMARINE

Aids clairvoyance, foresight, and spiritual awareness; promotes communication of spiritual insights; helps release

spiritual and emotional trauma; develops and balances fifth chakra qualities and soothes associated physical conditions (see Turquoise).

CALCITE

Strengthens memory, intellectual ability, and the physical mind; prepares physical and mental mind to receive higher mind; develops mental aspects of the seventh chakra and soothes associated physical conditions.

CITRINE

Develops self-discipline; helps assimilate experience and manifest innate creativity; taps naturally assertive energy of all kinds; energizes the physical body; supports the will; develops and balances third chakra qualities and soothes associated physical conditions.

DIAMOND

Offers protection of all kinds; provides identification with the immortal self; develops and balances seventh chakra qualities and associated physical conditions (see Quartz).

EMERALD

Soothes and strengthens the eyes; heals the energetic anatomy; promotes soul and heart awareness; calms emotions; taps innate capacities for love and prosperity; develops and balances fourth chakra qualities and soothes associated physical conditions (see Green Tourmaline).

FLUORITE

Accesses visionary insight and universal mind; protects against interferences with the human energy system (from radiation, TVs, computers); develops and balances the mental and physical aspects of seventh chakra qualities (see Amethyst and Calcite).

GARNET

Promotes use of creative energy; accesses vitality; develops and balances first and second chakra qualities and associated illnesses, including work with heart, blood, and circulatory system.

JADE

Encourages and supports dreamwork of all kinds, particularly that which helps achieve emotional release or accesses higher guidance; aids intuitive dream interpretation (see Quartz, Herkimer Diamond).

LAPIS LAZULI

Promotes clear sight of all kinds, including clairvoyance; removes illusions to access insight; calms the mind; develops wisdom; develops and balances sixth chakra qualities and associated conditions, including strengthening memory and eyesight (see Sapphire).

MALACHITE

Promotes emotional balance; accesses consciousness of soul and heart; dissolves emotional blocks; develops and balances fourth chakra qualities and associated conditions (see Green Tourmaline).

MOONSTONE

Promotes emotional balance and creative and intuitive work; stone of the Goddess; stone of the second chakra (see Garnet and Ruby).

OBSIDIAN

Promotes awareness of untapped potential; cleanses, grounds, focuses, and calms the self; associated with first chakra qualities and conditions (see Smoky Quartz).

OPAL

Promotes awareness of emotions; stimulates activity and change; generally associated with the versatility and vast resources of the seventh chakra, although can also be associated with the second (see Quartz). If one color dominates, its quality will influence these essential attributes. (Those who feel "unstable" should use only with extreme care.)

QUARTZ

Intensifies and focuses energy of all kinds (physical, mental, intuitive); by intention, can be programmed to take on the qualities and characteristics of any colored stone; energizes, harmonizes, heals, and expands capabilities of all bodies; develops awareness of seventh chakra qualities (particularly spiritual awareness) and balances associated conditions.

QUARTZ (HERKIMER DIAMOND)

Encourages and supports dreamwork of all kinds, particularly that involving astral travel and the reception of higher guidance (see Jade and Quartz).

QUARTZ (ROSE)

Develops joy and self-love; lifts depression; relieves stress; creates warmth; develops fourth chakra qualities and soothes associated physical conditions (see Pink Tourmaline).

QUARTZ (SMOKY)

Grounds, focuses, calms; develops first chakra qualities and soothes associated physical conditions (see Obsidian and Black Tourmaline).

RHODOCHROSITE

Infuses personal power and will (third chakra) with compassion (fourth chakra).

RUBY

Develops balanced sexual energies; develops self-worth; expands creative energy; develops and balances second chakra qualities and associated physical conditions, including work with heart, blood, and circulatory system (see Garnet).

SAPPHIRE

Soothes mind and spirit; aids intuitive work; develops sixth chakra qualities and associated physical conditions (see Lapis Lazuli).

TOPAZ

Promotes confidence in personal creativity; helps assimilate experience; increases energy, physical strength, and stamina; fortifies physical body for creative and spiritual work; balances neurological system; develops and balances third and sometimes second and seventh chakra qualities and associated physical conditions (see Citrine, Calcite).

TOURMALINE (BLACK)

Provides protection from negative influences; grounds (see Obsidian, Smoky Quartz).

TOURMALINE (BLUE)

Infuses communication with light; protects and fortifies the "voice" in all senses; relaxes throat area; increases clear communication of all kinds; stone of the fifth chakra (see Turquoise, Aquamarine).

TOURMALINE (GREEN)

Strengthens body to accept greater spirituality, charisma, radiance, and consciousness; increases prosperity, consciousness, and ability to love; cools fevers; rejuvenates on all levels; heals and protects; like quartz, can adapt to needs of the wearer; stone of the fourth chakra (see Malachite, Emerald).

TOURMALINE (PINK)

Infuses love with light; eases expression of love to others; inspires joy and enthusiasm for life; helps to release emotional pain; provides protection to wearer; stone of the fourth chakra.

TOURMALINE (WATERMELON)

Heals emotional wounds and supports new love simultaneously; stone of the fourth chakra.

TURQUOISE

Promotes clear communication; relaxes tension in jaw, throat, and mouth area; develops and balances fifth chakra qualities and associated physical conditions (see Aquamarine).

Numerology provides nine maps for nine universal paths toward wholeness and completion. These maps are also embodied in the universal symbols associated with each number. The symbols complement and illustrate the qualities of the numbers in graphic form.

In addition to numerology per se, sources like the Gnostic myth of Sophia, Egyptian texts, and Old and New Testament literature contain many numerical motifs. While sometimes they correspond, at other times they provide unique points of view.

1

Qualities: Originality, creativity, dynamism, vision, primordial unity, divinity, benevolence, protection

Symbols: Mandala, circle, rose or lotus blossom, infinite spiral

2

Qualities: Sensitivity, gentleness, artistry, detail, parenthood, introspection, devotion, charity, imagination

Symbol: Yin-yang

3

Qualities: Self-expression, joy, communication, imagination, friendship, community, education, optimism, expansion

Symbol: Equilateral triangle

4

Qualities: Method, craftsmanship, study, structure, work, sacrifice, realization of spirit in matter, salvation, manifestation of God on earth

Alternate interpretation: Individualism, originality, inventiveness, tolerance, genius, stubbornness

Symbols: Cross, pyramid (first interpretation of qualities)

5

Qualities: Change, intellect, communication, flexibility, travel, sensuality, adaptability, enthusiasm, versatility, the five stages of life (Birth, Initiation, Love, Repose, Death), resilience

Symbol: Pentagram

6

Qualities: Compassion, responsibility, aesthetics, family and teamwork, finance, pride, love and romance, courtesy

Symbol: Star of David

7

Qualities: Intuition, spirituality, faith, independence, wisdom, authority, solitude, mystery, receptivity, the quest

Symbol: Rainbow

8

Qualities: Determination, stamina, power, finance, authority, loyalty, ambition, wisdom through experience, patience, stability, caution, restriction, self-discipline

Symbol: Figure eight

9

Qualities: Humanitarianism, inspiration, daring, leadership, aggression, human life force, matter

Symbols: Chai' (Hebrew symbol for life: 18 = 2 × 9); The Alpha and the Omega

According to both esoteric tradition and modern physics, the human body actually consists of energy. This energy can be broken down into component parts, each of which has emotional, spiritual, and physical characteristics that combine to make a person. The body naturally draws on its life force energy and processes it through seven bodily energy centers, or chakras. This is a natural activity, like breathing. Eastern tradition teaches that you can strengthen the chakras through meditation, much as you can strengthen the lungs through physical exercise.

FIRST CHAKRA (ROOT, COCCYGEAL, OR MULADHARA)

Location: Base of spine

Attributes: Regulates survival instincts, vitality, sexuality, reproduction, and raw creativity (see Second Chakra).

Intuitive qualities: Source of intuitive self-protective instincts

Color: Red; when purified, white

Sound: Buzz

Experience: Kinesthetic and tactile

Nerve plexus: Sacral-coccygeal

Physiological system: Reproductive

Endocrine system: Gonads

Inadequate function can lead to: Blood disorders, infertility

SECOND CHAKRA (SACRAL, OR SWADHISTHANA)

Location: Spleen or navel

Attributes: Regulates emotional life, assimilation, and memories; in some systems, also regulates sexuality and raw creativity (see First Chakra).

Intuitive qualities: Can intuitively access key childhood experiences.

Color: Orange; in some systems, blue

Sounds: Ringing in the ears, running water

Experience: Emotional

Nerve plexus: Sacral

Physiological system: Genito-urinary

Endocrine system: Leydig

Inadequate function can lead to: Disorders of lungs and kidneys

THIRD CHAKRA (SOLAR PLEXUS, OR MANIPURA)

Location: Solar plexus

Attributes: Regulates balance, personal power, intellect.

Intuitive qualities: Associated with clairsentience, or psychic feeling.

Color: Golden yellow

Sound: Flute

Experience: Gut hunch

Nerve plexus: Solar

Physiological system: Digestive

Endocrine system: Adrenal glands

Inadequate function can lead to: Disorders of stomach, pancreas, and liver

FOURTH CHAKRA (HEART, OR ANAHATA)

Location: Center of chest

Attributes: Regulates compassion, growth, and inner harmony.

Intuitive qualities: Associated with clairsentience (see Third Chakra), psychic healing, and intuitive teaching skills.

Colors: Pink and green

Sounds: Singing, bells, roar of a seashell, shofar

Experience: Unconditional love

Nerve plexus: Heart plexus

Physiological system: Circulatory

Endocrine system: Thymus

Inadequate function can lead to: Heart disease or hypertension

FIFTH CHAKRA (THROAT, OR VISHUDDA)

Location: Hollow of throat

Attributes: Regulates creativity, self-expression, discipline, will.

Intuitive qualities: Associated with clairaudience (psychic hearing).

Color: Turquoise

Sound: Wind, ocean

Experience: Hearing or speaking

Nerve plexus: Cervical ganglia medulla

Physiological system: Respiratory

Endocrine system: Thyroid

Inadequate function can lead to: Thyroid and laryngeal diseases

SIXTH CHAKRA (THIRD EYE, OR AJNA)

Location: Between and slightly above the eyes

Attributes: Vision, intuition, imagination

Intuitive qualities: Associated with clairvoyance (psychic vision).

Color: Indigo

Sound: "Ohm" mantra

Experience: Sight or vision

Nerve plexus: Hypothalamus

Physiological system: Autonomic nervous system

Endocrine system: Pituitary

Inadequate function can lead to: Eye disorders

SEVENTH CHAKRA (CROWN, OR SAHASRARA)

Location: Very top of the head

Attributes: Regulates spiritual awareness and access to universal mind.

Intuitive qualities: Associated with prophecy (pure or "double" intuition).

Colors: White, pale lavender, violet

Sound: Silence

Experience: Receiving a whole concept

Nerve plexus: Cerebral cortex

Physiological system: Central nervous system

Endocrine system: Pineal

Inadequate function can lead to: Nervous and mental disorders

Six different layers of energy surround the human body. Together with the physical body, these are called the Seven Bodies. Each is the source of a different level of awareness. At this moment, much new intuitive research is being done on the topic. The demarcation between energetic bodies should not be taken too strictly; they are best regarded as a continuous spectrum.

Use the information below as a guide while filtering these ideas through your own experiences and intuition.

FIRST BODY OR PHYSICAL BODY

Source of: Physical functions; sensations; experiences

Appearance: The physical body

Heard at this level: Everyday sounds

Experience: Daily physical experience and consciousness

Quality of energy: Physical matter

Key phrase: I exist

SECOND BODY OR ETHERIC BODY

Source of: Love energy; sending of interdimensional messages; soul's karma; astrological influences; energy patterns that govern the form of the physical body

Appearance: Pale, shining blue

Heard at this level: Normal sounds heard keenly

Experience: Deep physical sensations; deeply intertwined with the physical body

Quality of energy: Physical sensations

Key phrase: I respond

THIRD BODY OR LOWER MENTAL BODY

Source of: Mental process; rational thought; linear thinking

Appearance: Yellow light

Heard at this level: Rhythmic beat

Experience: Cold and logical; without feeling or sensation

Quality of energy: Separated into subplanes or compartments

Key phrase: I think

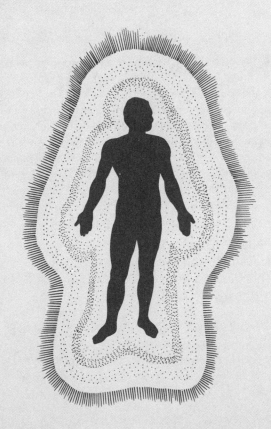

THE SEVEN BODIES

FOURTH BODY OR ASTRAL BODY

Source of: Dynamic emotion and desire; intense emotional experience of ourselves and others; vehicle for out-of-body travel

Appearance: Multicolored energy described as having characteristics of water or clouds

Experience: Emotional experience (including repression of emotions); profound unity of one's own emotions and experience of blending with feelings of another

Quality of energy: More sensitive; responds rapidly; enjoys change; has no space or time limitations

Key phrase: I am one with everyone

FIFTH BODY OR HIGHER MIND OR ETHERIC TEMPLATE

Source of: Higher or divine will; ability to differentiate and detail spiritual energies and communicate them to lower bodies; ability to create thought forms and to manifest them through words and sounds; awareness of responsibility for one's actions

Appearance: Cobalt blue space

Heard at this level: The voice within

Experience: Sense of mastery and strength; direct connection to higher forces and awareness

Quality of energy: Powerful focusing and physical follow-through of concrete thoughts and ideas; go-between among lower levels and higher self

Key phrase: I will

SIXTH BODY OR CAUSAL BODY

Source of: Higher self and access to sum total of wisdom attained in other lifetimes; universal love and compassion for all forms of energy and life; abstract ideas and concepts; essences and causes behind appearances

Appearance: Iridescent pastel light shot through with white and gold

Heard at this level: White noise or humming

Experience: Spiritual ecstasy (feeling level of spiritual plane)

Quality of energy: Peace and security

Key phrase: I know and love universally

SEVENTH BODY OR KETHERIC BODY

Source of: Higher mind; knowledge and integration of spiritual and physical aspects of the self

Appearance: Golden (sometimes seen as many golden threads); shaped like an eggshell

Heard at this level: White noise or humming

Experience: Peace, stillness, security

Quality of energy: Pure, strong source energy

Key phrase: I am

THE TREE OF LIFE

The Tree of Life with its ten sephiroth (spheres) charts out another map of energy, said to be the source of Western esoteric tradition, as the chakras are the source of the Eastern tradition. The sephiroth on the right side of the diagram belong to the positive pillar, called the Pillar of Mercy. This pillar is described as spirit, masculine, and active. The pillar on the left side of the diagram is called the Pillar of Severity and governs that which is material, negative, feminine, and passive. The central pillar is that of Equilibrium, or consciousness. The movement of the Tree of Life diagram is from top to bottom, as the primordial energy of Kether at the top evolves into the physical world of Malkuth at the bottom. This movement is expressed as a lightning flash that zigzags from pillar to pillar along the journey.

Although energy pools into spheres along the way, the essence of the Tree of Life lies in the interrelationship and dynamic balance of the individual sephiroth into a whole, just as the essence of the chakra system lies in the circulation of energy through all the chakras.

KETHER (THE CROWN)

Basic attribute: Highest of forces and primordial force
Part of the body: Head
Color: White

CHOKMAH (WISDOM)

Basic attribute: Active intelligence
Part of the body: Brain
Color: Gray or silver

BINAH (UNDERSTANDING)

Basic attribute: Receptive intelligence
Part of the body: Heart
Color: Black

CHESED (MERCY)

Basic attribute: Mercy
Part of the body: Right arm
Color: Blue

GEBURAH (JUDGMENT)

Basic attribute: Limiting strength

Part of the body: Left arm

Color: Red

TIPHERETH (BEAUTY)

Basic attribute: Highest perception of the divine presence we can have in earthly life

Part of the body: Chest

Color: Yellow

NETZACH (VICTORY)

Basic attribute: Eternal form

Part of the body: Right leg

Color: Green

CHOD (GLORY)

Basic attribute: Specific appearance and shape

Part of the body: Left leg

Color: Orange

JESOD (FOUNDATION)

Basic attribute: Power that generates the material world

Part of the body: Genitals

Color: Purple

MALKUTH (THE KINGDOM)

Basic attributes: Physical reality and humanity

Part of the body: Union of whole body

Colors: Brown, citrine, olive, black

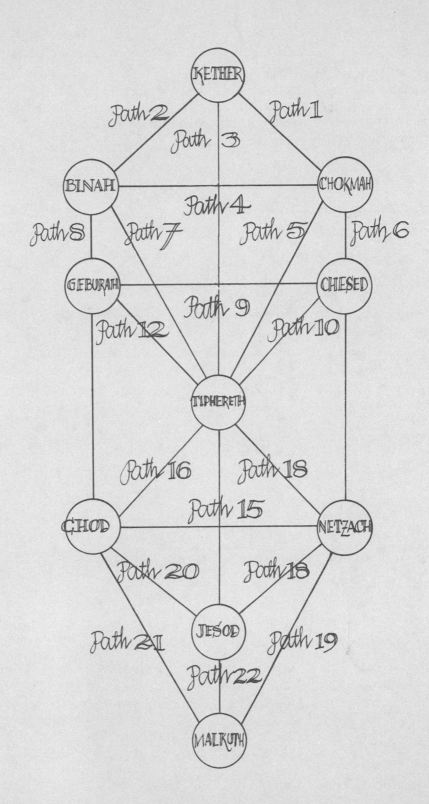

In Earth Traditions, the tool of growth and creation is often a great circle that raises power, provides growth experiences, and teaches awareness. The Four Directions are the focal points of energy and experience in these circles. We move between them to grow and live, and stand in the center to focus and strengthen our own power.

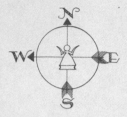

THE RELIGION OF THE GREAT GODDESS
(CIRCLE OF POWER)

DIRECTION: EAST

Element: Air

Correspondence: Mind

Time of day: Dawn

Season: Spring

Colors: Cool pastels, white, violet

Animal: Eagle

Power: Power to know

Tool: Sword

DIRECTION: SOUTH

Element: Fire

Correspondence: Energy or spirit

Time of day: Noon

Season: Summer

Colors: Red and orange

Animal: Lion

Power: Power to will or do

Tool: Wand or staff

DIRECTION: WEST

Element: Water

Correspondence: Feeling

Time of day: Dusk

Season: Autumn

Color: Blue, gray, sea green, deep purple

Animals: Fish and sea creatures

Power: Power to dare and courage

Tool: The Cup

DIRECTION: NORTH

Element: Earth

Correspondence: Mystery, the unseen, the body

Time of day: Midnight

Season: Winter

Colors: Brown, black, green of growth

Power: Power of silence and listening

Totems: Dark maiden and sacred bull

Tool: Pentacle

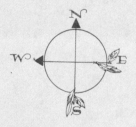

THE SIOUX FOUR DIRECTIONS

DIRECTION: EAST

Abode of: Sun, morning star, elk

Source of: Wisdom, understanding

Color: Yellow

Animals: Elk, golden eagle

Life stage: Old age, death, afterlife

DIRECTION: SOUTH

Abode of: Animal spirits

Source of: Life and destiny

Color: White

Animal: White crane

Life stage: Birth

DIRECTION: WEST

Abode of: The Thunder being and horse power

Source of: Purifying water

Color: Black

Animal: Black eagle

Life stage: Youth

DIRECTION: NORTH

Abode of: Calf pipe woman and buffalo

Source of: Health and control

Color: Red

Symbol: Bald eagle

Life Stage: Middle age

CHEYENNE MEDICINE WHEEL

DIRECTION: NORTHEAST

Abode of: Buffalo

Source of: Wisdom, silence, power, death, disease

Color: Black

DIRECTION: SOUTHEAST

Abode of: Eagle

Source of: Light, illumination, renewal, life

Color: White

DIRECTION: SOUTHWEST

Abode of: Mouse

Source of: Innocence, growth, weather

Color: Red

DIRECTION: NORTHWEST

Abode of: Bear

Source of: Introspection, perfection, beauty, harvest

Color: Yellow

In Chinese astrology, the creative principle is perceived as the five natural elements of a dynamic life cycle of birth, growth, and repose. Each element also corresponds to a season of the year.

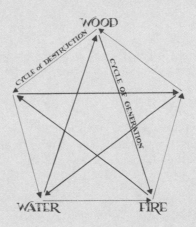

WOOD

Season: Growth and creation (or birth)

Generative force: Grows the fuel for the fire

Destructive force: Absorbs the goodness from the earth

Key words: Creativity, innovation

FIRE

Season: The hot season (or initiation)

Generative force: Burns the fuel into ash or earth

Destructive force: Melts metal

Key words: Stimulation, energy

EARTH

Season: Center of the year (or love)

Generative force: Provides the ground where metals are mined

Destructive force: Sullies water

Key words: Stability

METAL

Season: Harvest (or repose)

Generative force: Melts into liquid

Destructive force: Chops down wood

Key words: Valor, business, conflict

WATER

Season: The cold, wet season (or death)

Generative force: Feeds the growing wood

Destructive force: Quenches fire

Key words: Communication, intelligence, change

In classical Western astrology, the creative principle or life force is seen as the four natural elements—fire, earth, air, and water.

FIRE

Astrological signs: Aries, Leo, Sagittarius

Direction: South

Colors: Red, gold, orange

Motivation: Inspirational

Key words: Ardor, courage, creativity, enthusiasm, rashness, spontaneity, zeal

Planets: Sun, Mars, Jupiter

Tree: Almond tree in flower

Numbers: 1, 3, 4, 9

EARTH

Astrological signs: Taurus, Virgo, Capricorn

Direction: North

Colors: Black, brown, green, white

Motivation: Physical

Key words: Caution, conservatism, dependability, possessiveness, practicality, reliability, the body, growth, nature

Planets: Venus, Vulcan (undiscovered), Saturn

Tree: Oak

Numbers: 5, 6, 8

AIR

Astrological signs: Gemini, Libra, Aquarius

Direction: East

Colors: White, bright yellow, crimson, blue-white

Motivation: Mental

Key words: Alertness, curiosity, expression of ideas, intellect, perception, logic, knowledge, intuitive work

Planets: Mercury, Venus, Uranus

Tree: Aspen

Numbers: 4, 5, 6

WATER

Astrological signs: Cancer, Scorpio, Pisces

Direction: West

Colors: Blue, green, gray

Motivation: Emotional

Key words: Psychic perception, receptivity, responsiveness, sensitivity, subjectivity, fertility, the unconscious mind

Planets: Moon, Pluto, Neptune

Tree: Willow

Numbers: 2, 3, 7, 9

In the Seven Ray system as described by leading exponent Alice Bailey, pure creative energy refracts into seven rays of energy—each with a color and essential quality.

It is said that two rays predominate in each life: One is expressed by the soul or essence, and the other is expressed by the personality. Activities, objects, manmade events, the activity of nature, and all other forms of matter and energy also have one of the original seven rays as their essence and may be modified by other rays.

There is often more divergence in interpretations of the Seven Rays than in other esoteric systems, particularly in the area of color.

FIRST RAY

Symbol/esoteric master: The Father

Key words: Will and creativity/Tyranny and destruction

Can actualize as: The born leader

Astrological equivalent: Taurus, Pisces

Polarity: Positive

Color: Red; in some systems, white or blue

SECOND RAY

Symbol/esoteric master: The Son

Key words: Love-wisdom and supreme truth/Coldness, indifference

Can actualize as: The teacher or ambassador

Astrological equivalent: Leo, Sagittarius, Aquarius

Polarity: Negative

Color: Light blue; in some systems, pink or yellow

THIRD RAY

Symbol/esoteric master: The Holy Spirit or Trinity

Key words: Active intelligence or harmony through love/Isolation, selfishness

Can actualize as: The maker of forms

Astrological equivalent: Capricorn, Sagittarius

Polarity: Positive

Color: Yellow; in some systems, green or pink

FOURTH RAY

Symbol/esoteric master: The Hand of God, The Trumpet of the Lord

Key words: Harmony, beauty, creativity/Strong passions, indolence, self-centeredness

Can actualize as: The artist

Astrological equivalent:
Virgo, Gemini, Cancer,
Aries

Polarity: Negative

Color: Green; in some systems, white or yellow

FIFTH RAY

Symbol/esoteric master: The
Mind of God

Key words: Concrete
knowledge/Narrow-
mindedness

Can actualize as: The
scientist

Astrological equivalent:
Libra, Gemini, Taurus

Polarity: Positive

Color: Orange; in some
systems, rust or brown

SIXTH RAY

Symbol/esoteric master:
Jesus the Man

Key words: Devotion or
idealism/Dependence,
superstition

Can actualize as: The
devotee

Astrological equivalent:
Scorpio, Aries, Cancer

Polarity: Negative

Color: Ruby red, rose, silver; in some systems, blue
or indigo

SEVENTH RAY

Symbol/esoteric master: The
Unveiled Magician

Key words: Ceremony,
magic, and form/Pride, superficial judgment, bigotry

Can actualize as: The high
priest

Astrological equivalent:
Aquarius, Libra

Polarity: Positive

Color: Violet; in some systems, white

The Tarot is a deck of seventy-eight cards used to predict trends in life and to understand the archetypal energies within us. The order of trumps shown here is the order of the classic Tarot of Marseille. The astrological influences shown are from the British esoteric tradition. Some modern decks have made slight adjustments in order. The most common of these are shown in parentheses, as are classical astrological influences that were revised by the discovery of Neptune, Uranus, and Pluto in this century.

THE FOOL

Spiritual keys: Facing the
unexpected with trust and
spontaneity can lead to
wisdom, evolution, and
serenity.

Divinatory keys: The unexpected or opportunities or
changes in direction; the
necessity of facing the
unknown

Kabalistic path: Chokmah
to Kether

Chakra influence: Third eye
to crown

Astrological influence:
Uranus (or Air)

Musical note: E

Number: 0 (in some
decks 22)

Related myths or archetypes:
King Lear and his Fool,
Charlie Chaplin, Dionysus

THE MAGICIAN

Spiritual keys: Human will
and creativity can celebrate
divine energy in the world.

Divinatory keys: New vitality, new resolve, dexterity and intuitive powers;
new opportunities and the
wherewithal to master
them

Kabalistic path: Binah to
Kether

Chakra influence: Third eye
to crown

Astrological influence:
Mercury

Musical note: E

Number: 1

Related myths or archetypes:
Hermes as Magician

THE HIGH PRIESTESS

Spiritual keys: There is
much latent spiritual

wealth in the world to be
discovered and interpreted.

Divinatory keys: Heightened powers of intuition,
new discovery of the inner
self and its resources;
mother and nurturer of
spirit

Kabalistic path: Binah to
Kether

Chakra influence: Heart to
crown

Astrological influence:
Moon

Musical notes: G sharp/
A flat

Number: 2 (sometimes 4)

Related myths or archetypes:
Isis, Persephone

THE EMPRESS

Spiritual keys: What we
create from our natural
creativity and fertility will
help us grow spiritually.

Divinatory keys: Marriage
and creative partnerships of
any kind, the birth of a
child, period of high creative productivity or rewarding social activity

Kabalistic path: Binah to
Chokmah

Chakra influence: Third eye
passive to third eye active

Astrological influence:
Venus

Musical notes: F sharp/
G flat

Number: 3 (sometimes 2)

Related myths or archetypes:
Aphrodite, Demeter

THE EMPEROR

Spiritual keys: We have the
energy to give our structures and ideas material reality, which will help us
grow spiritually.

Divinatory keys: Call to

master and assimilate the father principle and authority structures, challenge to establish, evaluate, reform, or conquest an existing structure

Kabalistic path: Jesod to Netzach

Chakra influence: Navel to solar

Astrological influence: Aries

Musical note: C

Number: 4 (sometimes 3)

Related myths or archetypes: Zeus, the Arthurian Cycle

THE HIGH PRIEST

Spiritual keys: There is an obligation to communicate and carry out spiritual teachings and to have the material substance to convey such teachings.

Divinatory keys: Active intelligence, priesthood, metaphysics, religious or scientific vocation

Kabalistic path: Chesed to Chokmah

Chakra influence: Throat to third eye

Astrological influence: Taurus

Musical notes: C sharp/ D flat

Number: 5

Related myths or archetypes: The search for the Grail, the Last Supper

THE LOVERS

Spiritual keys: It is through physical love or aesthetic passion that we become one with the universe; experiencing polarities and making choices are basic parts of being human.

Divinatory keys: Need to make a careful choice, often in love or between

love and career or being creative; demonstrating a stronger love through separating oneself from a lesser love

Kabalistic path: Chesed to Chokmah

Chakra influence: Throat to third eye

Astrological influence: Gemini

Musical note: D

Number: 6

Related myths or archetypes: Judgment of Paris, the Dioscuri

THE CHARIOT

Spiritual keys: We grow spiritually as we master our passions.

Divinatory keys: Coming to grips with our passions, aggressions, and material desires can result in stronger personality; intelligence, balance, and philosophical approach can lead to victory

Kabalistic path: Geburah to Binah

Chakra influence: Throat to third eye

Astrological influence: Cancer

Musical note: D sharp/ E flat

Number: 7

Related myths or archetypes: Ares

JUSTICE

Spiritual keys: Judgment exercised with awareness, balance, and compassion is an expression of cosmic intelligence.

Divinatory keys: Need to make important decisions with perspective, balance, detachment, and compas-

sion; need to discover equilibrium of give and take in an existing situation

Kabalistic path: Tiphereth to Geburah

Chakra influence: Heart to throat

Astrological influence: Libra

Musical notes: F sharp/ G flat

Number: 8 (sometimes 11)

Related myths or archetypes: Pallas Athena

THE HERMIT

Spiritual keys: Patience and wisdom bring truth and clarity.

Divinatory keys: Withdrawal from social, group, or cultural activities or disregarding short-term, smaller needs for higher or long-term needs brings patience, which in turn brings solid foundations for the future.

Kabalistic path: Tiphereth to Chesed

Chakra influence: Heart to throat

Astrological influence: Virgo

Musical note: F

Number: 9 (sometimes 11)

Related myths or archetypes: Kronos, the private meetings of the Kings of the Arthurian Round Table

THE WHEEL OF FORTUNE

Spiritual keys: Card of karmic process; preparing for a new cycle of spiritual growth that is a direct consequence of the last cycle of spiritual growth

Divinatory keys: Sudden, fateful change of fortune, onset of new growth period in life

Kabalistic path: Netzach to Chesed

Chakra influence: Solar active to solar passive

Astrological influence: Jupiter

Musical note: B flat/ A sharp

Number: 10 (sometimes 12)

Related myths or archetypes: The Furies, the universal yearning that leads to the need to set out on the Quest

STRENGTH

Spiritual keys: Human power can be exercised in accordance with divine law.

Divinatory keys: Confrontation with the beast within or without; experiences of courage, strength, and self-discipline

Kabalistic path: Geburah to Chesed

Chakra influence: Solar passive to solar active

Astrological influence: Leo

Musical note: E

Number: 11 (sometimes 8 or 10)

Related myths or archetypes: Hercules, Daniel in the Lion's Den, Androcles and the Lion, Richard the Lionhearted

THE HANGED MAN

Spiritual keys: Sacrifice leads to greater goals; ceasing worldly work can lead to experience of inner truths.

Divinatory keys: Need to sacrifice something dear (for example, material security, attitude, or fantasy) to obtain something even more precious

Kabalistic path: Chod to Geburah

Chakra influence: Solar to throat

Astrological influence: Neptune (sometimes water)

Musical notes: G sharp/ A flat

Number: 12

Related myths or archetypes: Prometheus

DEATH

Spiritual keys: Profound transformation

Divinatory keys: Passage from one stage or cycle of life to another

Kabalistic path: Netzach to Tiphereth

Chakra influence: Solar to heart

Astrological influence: Scorpio

Musical note: G

Number: 13 (sometimes 14)

Related myths or archetypes: Pluto

TEMPERANCE

Spiritual keys: The process of adapting to a new activity to learn lessons or master spiritual energy is a universal human process.

Divinatory keys: Adaptation, balancing, or tempering of a relationship, creation, or situation; accessing the balance within

Kabalistic path: Jesod to Tiphereth

Chakra influence: Navel to heart

Astrological influence: Sagittarius

Musical notes: G sharp/ A flat

Number: 14 (sometimes 9)

Related myths or archetypes: Iris, Rainbow Bridge

THE DEVIL

Spiritual keys: To gain spiritual enlightenment, we must experience material or human existence on the lowest levels.

Divinatory keys: Confronting the shadow side, our unnecessary ties to the material world

Kabalistic path: Chod to Tiphereth

Chakra influence: Solar to heart

Astrological influence: Capricorn

Musical note: A

Number: 15

Related myths or archetypes: Pan

THE TOWER

Spiritual keys: Sometimes we must break down existing forms to access wisdom.

Divinatory keys: Disruption will bring enlightenment.

Kabalistic path: Chod to Tiphereth

Chakra influence: Solar to heart

Astrological influence: Mars (sometimes Aquarius)

Musical note: C

Number: 16

Related myths or archetypes: Tower of Babel, King Minos' Labyrinth

THE STAR

Spiritual keys: Spiritual guidance and universal principles are present in our lives.

Divinatory keys: Hope, inspiration, health, card of meditation

Kabalistic path: Tiphereth to Chokmah

Chakra influence: Heart to third eye

Astrological influence: Aquarius (sometimes Aries)

Musical notes: A sharp/ B flat

Number: 17

Related myths or archetypes: Tinker Bell, the Star of Bethlehem, Pandora

THE MOON

Spiritual keys: There is a bond between the physical and astral planes that can bring multiplicity, illusion, and complication.

Divinatory keys: Uncertainty, multiple meanings, latent powers and forces; dreams and intuition, the primitive, the unspoken powers of instinct and nature

Kabalistic path: Malkuth to Netzach

Chakra influence: Root to solar

Astrological influence: Pisces

Musical note: B

Number: 18

Related myths or archetypes: Hecate, Lilith

THE SUN

Spiritual keys: Enlightenment can be achieved through triumphs and worldly success that harmonize with universal law.

Divinatory keys: Worldly accomplishment and rewards, auspicious marriage or partnership, a period of clarity and trust

Kabalistic path: Jesod to Chod

Chakra influence: Navel to solar

Astrological influence: The Sun

Musical note: D

Number: 19

Related myths or archetypes: Apollo

THE LAST JUDGMENT

Spiritual keys: Call to spiritual awareness can bring out a review of worldly experiences.

Divinatory keys: Spiritual renewal or awakening, shift in consciousness, fruit is born of worldly seeds

Kabalistic path: Malkuth to Chod

Chakra influence: Root to solar

Astrological influence: Pluto (or Fire)

Musical note: C

Number: 20

Related myths or archetypes: Hestia, Hermes as Guide of Souls

THE WORLD

Spiritual keys: Worldly balance can be achieved by universal law, and mastery through harmony.

Divinatory keys: Fulfillment in all undertakings and harmony with others

Kabalistic path: Malkuth to Jesod

Chakra influence: Root to navel

Astrological influence: Saturn

Musical note: A

Number: 21

Related myths or archetypes: The Serpent Coiled Around the Egg (Ouroboros)

Early in this century, Carl Jung wrote about a universal but unnamed tool of inner development—the power that myths and archetypes have to enrich, heal, and teach us. The myths and archetypes below are divided into common categories of experience. Try sampling them when similar situations crop up or when you are trying to access or develop a similar quality in your life. Meditate about your favorites and the power they have to heal, empower, or enhance your life. Either consciously or unconsciously, the deep intuitive meaning they contain will percolate through you. Books by Jung, Robert Johnson, Jean Shinoda Bolen, and Liz Green, among others, can provide more detailed insight about how to use the power of myths and archetypes in your life. Consult the Reading List at the back of Inner Resources for specific titles of interest.

MYTHS

QUEST AND SELF-KNOWLEDGE

The Fool (Tarot)

Hymn of the Pearl (Gnostic)

Jason and the Golden Fleece (Greek)

The Judgment of Paris (Greek)

The Odyssey (Greek)

Parsifal and other Grail myths (medieval)

Sofia (Gnostic)

TRANSFORMATION

Death (Tarot)

Demeter and Persephone (Greek)

Gilgamesh (ancient Babylonian)

The Last Judgment (Tarot)

Paul of Tarsis (ancient Near Eastern)

CREATIVITY AND FERTILITY

Aphrodite (Greek)

Changing Woman (Apache)

Clytemnestra (Greek)

Daedalus and Icarus (Greek)

Dionysus (Greek)

The Empress (Tarot)

Medusa (Greek)

Morgan le Fay (Arthurian cycle)

Orpheus (Greek)

The World (Tarot)

MEETING THE SHADOW SELF

The Chariot (Tarot)

The Devil (Tarot)

Jesus in the desert (ancient Near Eastern)

Joseph wrestling with the Angel (ancient Near Eastern)

The Lord of the Rings (modern)

The Mabingoen (Celtic)

Strength (Tarot)

SPIRITUAL AWAKENING, SPIRITUAL LIFE, DEVOTION

Augustine of Hippo (early Christian)

Cassandra (Greek)

The High Priest (Tarot)

The High Priestess (Tarot)

Hymn of the Pearl (Gnostic)

Isis (Egyptian)

Joan of Arc (medieval)

Job (ancient Near Eastern)

The Kathopanishad (Hindu)

Paul of Tarsis (ancient Near Eastern)

SACRIFICE

Abraham and Isaac (ancient Near Eastern)

Alcestis (Greek)

Demeter and Persephone (Greek)

The Hanged Man (Tarot)

Iphigenia (Greek)

Jesus (ancient Near Eastern)

Prometheus (Greek)

SURRENDER/LOSS OF INNOCENCE

Adam and Eve (ancient Near Eastern)

Antigone (Greek)

Atalanta and the Golden Apples (Greek)

Camelot (Arthurian cycle)

Hymn of the Pearl (Gnostic)

The Iliad (Greek)

Parsifal and other Grail myths (medieval)

The Tower (Tarot)

The Wheel of Fortune (Tarot)

RELATIONSHIP/ MARRIAGE/ PARTNERSHIP

Abraham and Sarah (ancient Near Eastern)

Hera and Zeus (Greco-Roman)

The Lovers (Tarot)

ROMANTIC LOVE

Echo and Narcissus (Greek)

The Judgment of Paris/ Helen of Troy (Greek)

Lancelot and Guinevere (Arthurian cycle)

The Lovers (Tarot)

Odysseus and Penelope (Greek)

Psyche and Eros (Greek)

Solomon and Bathsheba (ancient Near Eastern)

Temperance (Tarot)

BROTHERS

Cain and Abel (ancient Near Eastern)

Castor and Pollux (Greek)

BROTHER AND SISTER

Apollo and Artemis (Greek)

Orestes and Electra (Greek)

PARENT AND CHILD

Demeter and Persephone (Greek)

The Oresteia (Greek)

Thetis and Achilles in the Iliad (Greek)

Zeus and Athena (Greek)

ARCHETYPES

THE ARTIST

Aphrodite (Greek)
Daedalus (Greek)
Dionysus (Greek)
The Empress (Tarot)
The Magician (Tarot)
Orpheus (Greek)

THE HEALER

Hermes (Greek)
The High Priestess (Tarot)
Isis (ancient Near Eastern)
Orpheus (Greek)

SOLITUDE/INNER PEACE

Artemis (Greek)
The Hermit (Tarot)
Hestia (Greek)
Kronos (Greek)
The Last Judgment (Tarot)

THE MESSENGER

Cassandra (Greek)
Hermes as healer (Greek)
Iris (Greek)
Temperance (Tarot)

THE WARRIOR

Ares (Greek)
Athena (Greek)
The Chariot (Tarot)
Justice (Tarot)
Monster Slayer (Navajo)

THE BUILDER

The Emperor (Tarot)
Hephaestus the Forger (Greek)
King Minos and the Minotaur (Greek)

THE INTUITIVE

Cassandra (Greek)

Hermes as magician (Greek)
The High Priestess (Tarot)
Isis (Egyptian)
Joseph (ancient Near Eastern)
The Moon (Tarot)
Pandora (Greek)
Persephone (Greek)

INSPIRATION

Pegasus (Greek)
The Seven Muses (Greek)
The Star (Tarot)
The Three Muses (Greek)

Enter your personal patterns and symbols here. You might want to use each quadrant of space to list a different kind of symbol.

Consultation with: _____

Specialty: _____

Date: _____

Notes: _____

_____

_____

_____

_____

_____

_____

_____

_____

_____

_____

_____

Consultation with: _____

Specialty: _____

Date: _____

Notes: _____

_____

_____

_____

_____

_____

_____

_____

_____

_____

Abraham, Kurt. *Introduction to the Seven Rays*. Cape May, N.J.: Lampus Press.

Allende, Isabel. *The House of the Spirits*. Trans. by Magda Bogin. New York: Bantam, 1986.

Andrews, Edward Deming. *The Gift to be Simple*. New York: Dover, 1940.

Andrews, Lynn V. *Flight of the Seventh Moon*. New York: Harper and Row, 1984.

———. *Jaguar Woman*. New York: Harper and Row, 1985.

———. *Medicine Woman*. New York: Harper and Row, 1981.

———. *Star Woman*. New York: Warner, 1986.

An Anthology of Jewish Mysticism. Trans. by Raphael Ben Zion. New York: Judaica, 1981.

Auerbach, Erich. *Mimesis*. Princeton: Princeton University Press, 1953.

Augustine. *Confessions*. Trans. by R. S. Pine-Coffin. New York: Penguin, 1961.

Aurelius, Marcus. *Meditations*. Trans. by Maxwell Stanforth. New York: Penguin, 1984.

Avery, Jeanne. *Astrology and Your Past Lives*. New York: Fireside, 1987.

Bailey, A. A. *Esoteric Astrology*. New York: Lucis, 1951.

The Bhagavad Gita. Trans. by Franklin Edgerton. Cambridge: Harvard University Press, 1944.

Black Elk Speaks. Lincoln: University of Nebraska, 1961.

Blake, William. *The Portable Blake*. Ed. by Alfred Kazin. New York: Penguin, 1946.

Blofeld, John. *The Tantric Mysticism of Tibet*. New York: Dutton, 1970.

Blum, Ralph. *The New Book of Runes*. New York: St Martin's Press, 1982, 1987.

Bolen, Jean Shinoda. *Goddesses in Everywoman*. New York: Harper and Row, 1984.

Bradley, Marion Zimmer. *The Mists of Avalon*. New York: Del Ray, 1982.

Brand, Stewart. *The Media Lab*. New York: Viking, 1987.

Brennan, Barbara Ann. *Hands of Light*. New York: Bantam, 1988.

Brook, Stephen, ed. *The Oxford Book of Dreams*. Oxford: Oxford University Press, 1987.

Brown, Malcolm W. "Mathematics And Magic," in *The New York Times Magazine*, October 18, 1987.

Bry, Adelaide. *Visualization*. New York: Barnes and Noble, 1979.

Burt, Kathleen. *Astrology and Archetype*. St. Paul: Llewellyn, 1988.

Cainer, Jonathan, and Carl Rider. *The Psychic Explorer*. New York: Fireside, 1986.

Campbell, Joseph. *Creative Mythology*. New York: Penguin, 1968.

———. *Hero with a Thousand Faces*. Princeton: Princeton University Press, 1949.

———. *Occidental Mythology*. New York: Penguin, 1968.

———. *Oriental Mythology*. New York: Penguin, 1962.

Capra, Fritjof. *The Tao of Physics*. New York: Bantam, 1976.

Carlson, Ron. *The News of the World*. New York: Penguin, 1987.

Carroll, Lewis. *Alice in Wonderland*. New York: Doubleday, 1942.

Castaneda, Carlos. *The Teachings of Don Juan*. New York: Washington Square Press, 1968.

Cavafy, Constantine. *The Complete Poems of Cavafy*. Trans. by Rae Dalven. New York: Harcourt, Brace, Jovanovich, 1948.

Chandley, Margo. *The Channeling Process*. San Jose, Calif.: Sound and Light Communications, 1987.

Daly, Mary. *Beyond God the Father*. Boston: Beacon Press, 1973.

Dante. *Paradiso*. Trans. by Allen Mandelbaum. New York: Bantam, 1986.

de Bary, William Theodore, ed. *The Buddhist Tradition*. New York: Vintage, 1969.

Doane, Doris Chase, and King Keyes. *How to Read Tarot Cards*. New York: Barnes and Noble, 1979.

Dodge, Ellin. *You Are Your Birthday*. New York: Fireside, 1986.

———. *You Are Your First Name*. New York: Fireside, 1986.

Einstein, Albert. *Cosmic Religion*. New York: Covici, Friede, 1931.

———. *The World as I See It*. New York: Covici, Friede, 1934.

Einstein, Patricia. *Uncommon Sense*. New York: Villard, 1988.

Elkins, Dan, Carla Rueckert, and James Allen McCarty. *The Ra Material*. Norfolk: The Donning Company, 1984.

Garfield, Laeh Maggie. *Sound Medicine*. Berkeley, Calif.: Celestial Arts, 1987.

Garfield, Laeh Maggie, and Jack Grant. *Companions in Spirit*. Berkeley, Calif.: Celestial Arts, 1984.

Gawain, Shakti. *Creative Visualization*. San Rafael, Calif.: New World, 1978.

Gerber, Richard, M.D. *Vibrational Medicine*. Santa Fe, N.M.: Bear & Co., 1988.

Gibran, Kahlil. *The Prophet*. New York: Alfred A. Knopf, 1971.

Gleik, James. *Chaos*. New York: Viking, 1987.

Graham, A. C., ed. *Poems of the Late T'ang*. New York: Penguin, 1965.

Grant, Patrick, ed. *A Dazzling Darkness: An Anthology of Western Mysticism*. Grand Rapids, Mich.: Eerdsmans, 1985.

Gray, Eden. *Mastering the Tarot*. New York: Signet, 1971.

Greene, Liz. *The Astrology of Fate*. York Beach: Samuel Weiser, 1984.

Griscom, Chris. *Time Is an Illusion*. New York: Fireside, 1986.

Haitch, Elisabeth. *Initiation*. Palo Alto, Calif.: Seed Center, 1974.

Hardy, Thomas. *Far From the Madding Crowd*. New York: Scholastic, 1968.

Harris, Lis. *Holy Days*. New York: Summit, 1986.

Hay, Louise L. *You Can Heal Your Life*. Santa Monica, Calif.: Hay House, 1984.

Hightower, Dianna. "Ancient Teachings for the Modern World." *Meditation* 2, no. 4 (Fall 1987).

Hoffman, Edward. *The Way of Splendor*. Boston: Shambhala, 1981.

The Holy Bible. Revised Standard Version. New York: New American Library, 1962.

Huffines, LaUna. *Bridge of Light*. New York: Fireside 1988.

Hughes, Langston. *Selected Poems*. New York: Alfred A. Knopf, 1948.

I Ching. Ed. by Raymond Van Owen. New York: New American Library, 1971.

James, William. *The Varieties of Religious Experience*. New York: New American Library, 1958.

Johansen, Gayle, M.A., and Shinan Noam Barclay, Ph.D. *The Sedona Vortex Experience*. Sedona: Sunlight, 1987.

Johnson, Robert. *He*. King of Prussia, Pa.: Religious Publishing Company, 1974.

Jonas, Hans. *The Gnostic Religion*. Boston: Beacon, 1958.

Jung, C. G. *Man and His Symbols*. New York: Doubleday, 1964.

———. *Memories, Dreams, Reflections*. New York: Random House, 1961.

———. *The Portable Jung*. Ed. by Joseph Campbell. New York: Penguin, 1971.

Kalweit, Holger. *Dreamtime & Inner Space*. Boston: Shambhala, 1988.

Klimo, Jon. *Channeling*. Los Angeles: Jeremy P. Tarcher, 1987.

Knight, Gareth. *A Practical Guide to Qabalistic Symbolism*. York Beach, ME: Samuel Weiser, 1965.

Krieger, Dolores, Ph.D., R.N. *The Therapeutic Touch*. Englewood Cliffs, N.J.: Prentice Hall, 1979.

Lao Tzu. *Tao Te Ching*. Trans. by D. C. Lau. New York: Penguin, 1963.

Larousse Encyclopedia of Greek and Roman Mythology. Paris: Larousse, 1965.

Le Guin, Ursula K. *The Earthsea Trilogy: A Wizard of Earthsea; The Tombs of Atuan; The Farthest Shore*. New York: Bantam, 1968, 1975, 1975.

L'Engle, Madeleine. *A Wrinkle in Time*. New York: Dell, 1962.

Lineman, Rose, and Jan Popelka. *Compendium of Astrology*. West Chester, Pa.: Para Research, 1984.

Lowary-Petersen, Sheila. *The Fifth Dimension*. New York: Fireside, 1988.

Luckert, Karl W. *Navajo Mountain and Rainbow Bridge Religion*. Flagstaff, Ariz.: Museum of Northern Arizona, 1977.

Machiavelli, Niccolo. *The Prince and the Discourses*. Trans. by Luigi Ricci. New York: Modern Library, 1950.

MacLaine, Shirley. *Dancing in the Light*. New York: Bantam 1985.

Mails, Thomas E. *Secret Native American Pathways*. Tulsa: Council Oak Books, 1988.

Mann, Thomas. *The Magic Mountain*. Trans. by H. T. Lowe-Porter. New York: Random House, 1957.

Mansfield, Katherine. *Journal*. Ed. by J. Middleton Murray. New York: Ecco, 1933.

Meltzer, David. *The Secret Garden: An Anthology in the Kabbalah*. New York: Seabury, 1976.

Munro, Eleanor. *On Glory Roads*. New York: Thames and Hudson, 1987.

Murdoch, Iris. *The Good Apprentice*. New York: Viking Penguin, 1985.

Nabokov, Vladimir. *Speak, Memory*. New York: Perigee, 1947.

Neal, V., and S. Karagulla. *Through the Curtain*. DeVorss and Company, 1983.

Nicholson, Shirley, ed. *Shamanism*. Wheaton, IL: The Theosophical Publishing Company, 1987.

Ouseley, S.G.J. *The Power of the Rays*. Heath: Fowler.

Peck, M. Scott, M.D. *The Road Less Travelled*. New York: Touchstone, 1978.

Pirsig, Robert M. *Zen and the Art of Motorcycle Maintenance*. New York: Morrow, 1974.

Rama, Swami. *Life Here and Hereafter*. Honesdale: Himalayan Publishers, 1976.

Randolph, Vance. *Ozark Magic and Folklore*. New York: Dover, 1947.

Raphaell, Katrina. *Crystal Enlightenment*. Santa Fe, NM: Aurora, 1985.

———. *Crystal Healing*. Santa Fe, NM: Aurora, 1987.

Richie, Donald. *Zen Inklings*. New York: Weatherhill, 1982.

Roberts, Jane. *Adventures in Consciousness*. New York: Bantam, 1984.

———. *The Adventures of Oversoul Seven*. Englewood Cliffs, N.J.: Prentice Hall, 1973.

———. *The Further Education of Oversoul Seven*. Englewood Cliffs, N.J.: Prentice Hall, 1979.

Roethke, Theodore. *Collected Poems*. Garden City, N.Y.: Doubleday, 1937.

Rohde, Eleanor Sinclair. *A Garden of Sundry Herbs*. New York: Dover, 1936.

Roman, Sanaya, and Duane Packer. *Opening to Channel.* Tiburon: H. J. Kramer, 1987.

Rothenberg, Jerome, and George Quasha, eds. *America, A Prophecy.* New York: Vintage, 1973.

Scholem, Gershon. *The Messianic Idea in Judaism.* Trans. by Michael Meyer and Hillel Hankin. New York: Schocken, 1978.

Shakespeare, William. *The Riverside Shakespeare.* Ed. by G. Blakemore Evans. Boston: Houghton Mifflin, 1974.

Sharman-Burke, Juliet, and Liz Greene. *The Mythic Tarot.* New York: Fireside, 1986.

Shin, Florence Scovell. *The Game of Life.* New York: Fireside, 1925.

Shin, Nan. *Diary of a Zen Nun.* New York: Dutton: 1986.

Siegel, Bernie S., M.D. *Love, Medicine, & Miracles.* New York: Harper and Row, 1988.

Silbey, Uma. *The Complete Crystal Guidebook.* San Francisco: U-Read, 1986.

Spiller, Jan, and Karen McCoy. *Spiritual Astrology.* New York: Fireside, 1988.

Starhawk. *The Spiral Dance.* Boston: Beacon Press, 1979.

Steinbrecher, Edwin C. *The Inner Guide Meditation.* York Beach, ME: Samuel Weiser, 1988.

Stevens, Jose, Ph.D., and Lena Stevens. *Secrets of Shamanism.* New York: Avon, 1988.

Strayhorn, Lloyd. *Numbers and You.* New York: Ballantine, 1980.

Sugrue, Thomas. *There Is a River: The Story of Edgar Cayce.* Virginia Beach: ARE, 1942.

TeSelle, Sallie. *Speaking in Parables.* Philadelphia: Fortress, 1975.

Thoreau, Henry David. *Great Short Works by Henry David Thoreau.* Ed. by Wendell Flock. New York: Harper and Row, 1982.

The Tibetan Book of the Dead. Ed. by W. Y. Evanz-Wentz. Oxford: Oxford University Press, 1960.

Triangles. Lucis Trust. P.O. Box 722 Cooper Station, New York, N.Y. 10276

Trimble, Stephen, Harvey Lloyd, and the Indian Peoples of the Southwest. *Our Voices, Our Land.* Flagstaff: Northland, 1986.

Tweedie, Irina. *Daughter of Fire.* Nevada City: Blue Dolphin, 1986.

Uyldert, Millie. *The Magic of Precious Stones.* Great Britain: Turnstone, 1981.

Walters, Derek. *Ming Shu: The Art and Practice of Chinese Astrology.* New York: Fireside, 1988.

Watts, Alan. *In My Own Way.* New York: Vintage, 1972.

Weiss, Brian, M.D. *Many Lives, Many Masters.* New York: Fireside, 1988.

Wordsworth, William. *Selected Poems and Prefaces.* Ed. by Jack Stillinger. Boston: Houghton Mifflin, 1965.

Yeats, W. B. *The Collected Poems.* New York: Macmillan, 1956.

———. *A Vision.* New York: Macmillan, 1937.

Yogananda, Paramahansa. *Autobiography of a Yogi.* Los Angeles: Self-Realization Fellowship, 1946.

———. *Inner Reflections 1988.* Los Angeles: Self-Realization Fellowship, 1988.

Zohar. Trans. by Daniel Chanan Matt. Mahwah, N.J.: Paulist Press, 1983.

Would you like to share Inner Voyager entries, questions, and insights? Do you have any favorite exercises, quotes, review questions, or ideas for Inner Resources that you would like to see in a future edition of Inner Voyager? Please write: Inner Voyager, 217 East 86th Street, Suite 266, New York, NY 10028